"In an age of ambiguity and apathy for the church, *Total Church* accurately and insightfully identifies the local church as a gospel community on mission with Jesus."
—MARK DRISCOLL, Founding Pastor,
Mars Hill Church, Seattle

"Challenging, passionate and insightful. Here is a vision of a whole-life, whole-mission 'Total Church' that embraces both gospel and community—I suspect rather like it was all meant to be!"
—CHRIS STODDART, Director,
Reaching the Unchurched Network

"Here is radical, punchy teaching that provokes, stimulates, challenges and inspires. Its call for a dual fidelity to the gospel word and the gospel community is urgently needed for the health of our churches and the integrity of our mission."
—VAUGHAN ROBERTS, Rector, St Ebbe's Church, Oxford

"I have to confess to reading *Total Church* in one sitting! I found it very relevant to our situation in particular, and to the wider scene in general. *Total Church* digs deep and provides a solid biblical foundation for what it advocates. The argument of the book is very compelling and at the same time very practical. It has confirmed for me the need to multiply churches and has further convinced me of the need to downsize church and to think local. I am looking forward to seeing this book in print so that we can use it with our leaders as a training tool."
—DAVID JONES, Senior Minister,
Cornerstone Church, Hobart, Tasmania

"Reformed theology and new ways of being church are often regarded as incompatible notions. In this book, Tim Chester and Steve Timmis aim to bring the two together in a way that they believe will help church leaders identify ways of relating a conservative theology to the culture, without compromising dearly held principles."
—JOHN DRANE, freelance consultant to churches in the UK
and Professor of Practical Theology at Fuller Seminary,
California

"There is an old joke about a visitor to Ireland who, on stopping to ask a local the way to Dublin, was told, 'If I was going to Dublin, I wouldn't start here!' I often feel like this hapless visitor when I read books offering panaceas for the problems of the local church. But here is a book which starts where you are—and wherever you are—whether it be in a handful of people meeting in a home, or (as in my case) a congregation of a thousand people meeting in a traditional building, and offers directions for (in the words of the subtitle), 'A Radical Reshaping around Gospel and Community.' Written not by armchair experts but by ('dirty!') hands-on practitioners Tim Chester and Stephen Timmis, *Total Church* explores what it means in practice to be both gospel-centered and community-centered. Not everyone will agree with everything that is written, but every thoughtful reader and church leader will be stimulated to rethink and maybe reshape their 'default' practices and convictions. In my own setting, it reinforced a growing conviction that the only way in which you can be a meaningful part of a large church is to transition from being a church with small groups to a church of small groups, for (to quote from the book), 'People need to encounter the church as a network of relationships rather than a meeting you attend or a place you enter.' This would be an excellent book to give to your leaders, and to the wider church membership, to provoke discussion and prompt change. It will certainly set you in the right direction 'to Dublin'—from wherever you are!"
—PETER J. GRAINGER, Senior Minister,
Charlotte Chapel, Edinburgh

R | RE:LIT

total CHURCH

A Radical Reshaping
around Gospel
and Community

Tim Chester and Steve Timmis

CROSSWAY BOOKS
WHEATON, ILLINOIS

Library of Congress Cataloging-in-Publication Data
Chester, Tim.
   Total church : a radical reshaping around gospel and community /
Tim Chester and Steve Timmis.
     p. cm.
   Includes bibliographical references and index.
   ISBN 978-1-4335-0208-8 (tpb)
    1. Church. I. Timmis, Steve, 1957–   . II. Title
BV600.3.C44   2008
262.001'7—dc22   2008019147

VP   17   16   15   14   13   12   11   10   09   08
15   14   13   12   11   10   9   8   7   6   5   4   3   2   1

To
all our brothers and sisters
in The Crowded House
"You are our glory and joy"
1 Thessalonians 2:20

And to
Maurice Withington
one of God's true gentle men

CONTENTS

FOREWORD

YOU CAN TELL A LOT about people by their friends. I suspect that for many unchurched and non-churched, the same is true of Jesus. And as uncomfortable as it may sound, people form their views about Christ by looking at those who wear his name as a badge.

Hiding behind the defense "Don't look at us—look at Jesus" just won't wash. Truth be told, judging by church attendance statistics in the United Kingdom, for example, they are looking at us, then choosing not to bother with Jesus.

The authors of this book have spotted the problem and in their own way have set about a course of action to turn things around. They are part of a Christian community in northern England that goes by the name The Crowded House. It is a brave attempt to do church differently, not for the sake of trendy trailblazing, but as a serious exercise in doing Christian mission in a postmodern world. They are attempting to live out the gospel of Christ in the context of a local neighborhood and, by so doing, to draw others to personal, living faith. They are trying to be a different kind of church with a sort of easy-to-see, easy-to-understand, come-and-join-us feel. The book you are holding in your hand is just one product of this journey of faith.

There are several reasons why the wider church should thank Tim Chester and Steve Timmis for their efforts. First, this is a *relevant* book, as the topic of the shape and priorities of the church in the third millennium has filled a few bookshelves already. As one who has made a small contribution to that discussion, I welcome additional voices who add some fresh notes. But I am particularly glad that it is a book that is *down-to-earth* and avoids the trap of dealing in theories that sound cool in a classroom but crash on the ground. This is written by practitioners—and it shows.

I found it a *provocative* book to read, and I use the word in a healthy, faith-stretching way. I don't agree with all their arguments and conclusions (and think at times they need to engage with a wider constituency), but I love books that make me answer back like this one did. (Out loud and on a plane as well. Quite embarrassing.)

I appreciated the *honesty* of their writing, which freely acknowledges it is about principles and vision rather than a description of perfect practice. That kind of honesty connects with those of us who live with the mess of local church, because we know we are reading the words of realists who have learned to live with ragged edges. It was also good to gain some *warmth* of spiritual fervor, which seems in too many places to have fallen into disrepute. We desperately need a recovery of genuine enthusiasm from those who live *en-theos* ("in God," the root of the word).

The authors share the view of the late Lesslie Newbigin that the local congregation is "the hermeneutic of the gospel" (if you want to know what Jesus is like, look at the church). And here is their brave attempt to inspire us to look more like the Bride of Christ and less like the Bride of Frankenstein.

I believe it was John Stott who challenged the church to engage in the task of contextualizing the gospel—not to throw the baby out with the bathwater. Instead, he urged, we should keep the baby (the heart of the gospel) but change the bathwater (the way we "do church" in a given cultural context).

Well, Mr. Chester and Mr. Timmis aim to keep the baby but give it a whole new bathroom. And it's well worth a look.

Ian Coffey
Geneva, February 2007

ACKNOWLEDGMENTS

A BIG THANK-YOU TO Katy Jones Parry and Jen Baxter for their faithful assistance throughout, and the students of the Northern Training Institute for additional research. Thanks also to Steve McAlpine for the case studies. A number of people within The Crowded House network commented on the manuscript and suggested additional material. Thank you also to everyone at IVP: Brian Wilson who first suggested we write on this theme and Eleanor Trotter who guided us through the process with her usual skill. And a particular thank-you to our wives, Janet and Helen, for their unfailing help and companionship, and to our families for allowing us the time to write.

So much of this material has been developed in conversations and discussions within The Crowded House and beyond. It is truly the product of a community rather than two people, an example of the community hermeneutic we describe in Chapter 10. And so it seems appropriate to dedicate it to our community of communities. It is a privilege beyond telling to strive "side by side [with you] for the faith of the gospel" (Philippians 1:27 ESV).

INTRODUCTION

ALAN IS THE LEADER OF A small Baptist church. He moved to lead his suburban congregation five years ago after several years working in industry and three years studying in a theological college. He has seen a number of people join the church, but not as many as he had hoped. They have a thriving mothers-and-toddlers' group, a solid youth work program, and an accomplished music group. And yet Alan can't help feeling that the church is only scratching the surface. Truth be told, it feels as if ministry has become a production line: churning out sermons, putting on events, trying to generate another wave of enthusiasm for evangelism. If only there were a different way of doing church.

Bob was converted as a teenager in a lively Anglican church, then became a youth group leader. Now he no longer goes to church. It had just become a burden, a set of responsibilities. He was always being asked to do things. If he didn't show up at meetings, questions were asked and eyebrows raised. Conflict among church members was the last straw. "I don't need this," he told his wife the day he stopped going. He still reads his Bible, still prays, still tells unbelievers about Jesus if it comes up in conversation. "I'm just taking a break from church," he says. He can sense the disapproval when he runs into other Christians. He feels it himself. He knows Christians should be part of a church. But he can't face going back. If only there were a different way of doing church.

Cathy became a Christian in her first year at university. It was great. She spent hours hanging out with her Christian friends, talking through their faith, praying together, sharing the gospel with other students. But two years after graduation she feels spiritually flat. She goes to church each Sunday and attends a home group on Wednesday evenings. But she misses the intimacy of the relationships she had at university. She misses the discussions, the enthusiasm, and the late-night prayers. She laughs to herself at how immature they were sometimes. But she can't help wondering whether "grown-up" Christianity is any better. If only there were a different way of doing church.

Denzel was one of the founders of Elevate. Elevate grew out of a common desire to explore new ways of doing church. They were inspired by the alternative worship scene and some people within the emerging church movement. It started as a monthly gathering with images, incense, and meditations. From that came a weekly meeting in a pub. It was all very exciting at first. It still is. Denzel enjoys the energy that comes from doing something different. But he has some concerns. He suspects the Bible is not as central as it should be. Plus, although a number of other disaffected Christians have joined them, they don't seem to be impacting unbelievers. And then last week several members questioned whether adherents of other religions really need evangelizing. They talked about a safe place to ask questions, but Denzel felt uneasy. He thinks they're really on to something, and he certainly doesn't want to go back to a hymn sandwich and a sermon. But increasingly he worries about what is being sacrificed. If only there were a different way of doing church.

These people are fictional, but their stories are all based on real conversations and real experiences.

THE AUTHORS' STORIES

Maybe you can relate to Steve's story. Steve was the minister of a church in a working-class community in northern England. It was his first "charge," and it was something of a baptism by fire! The church was welcoming and caring, small and intimate. Looking back, despite all the early difficulties, it is hard to imagine a better place for a young man to be nurtured in ministry. The people loved the Lord and showed it in their love for his word and his people. Over time, the church grew as lives were changed by grace.

But for all that was good, Steve had a nagging sense of unease. The building was nearly full, but there were thousands outside. It was difficult to put his finger on it, but somehow so much of their life together as a church was inaccessible and irrelevant to those around. They loved each other, and the Bible was being taught, but he was growing increasingly aware of the almost impenetrable wall between the church and the world. It impacted traffic in both directions.

As Steve reflected, he saw two issues. First, for all the attempts at preaching God's word in a faithful and contemporary way, there was little opportunity for non-Christians to hear it. Second, although Steve was convinced that theirs was a believing community loving one other, there was little opportunity for non-Christians to be exposed to it. If only there were a different way of doing church.

Tim's story is different. He was brought up as a "pastor's kid." In his late teens his father was asking big questions about what it meant to be the church. Tim remembers long conversations as people shared their dreams about what church could be. At university he got the chance to make something of those dreams. He lived in a house with other Christians—eating together, worshipping together, offering hospitality, sharing lives. He has vivid memories of sitting around a large, battered, old table with the remnants of a meal and celebrating Communion together.

But life was very different after graduation when Tim and his wife, Helen, moved to north London. Tim still remembers the first time they were invited out for a meal. They assumed it would be that evening or maybe the next day. But a date three weeks away was suggested. It turned out to be their first experience of a "dinner party." It certainly wasn't sharing lives. If only there were a different way of doing church.

KEY PRINCIPLES

This book argues that two key principles should shape the way we "do church": gospel and community. Christians are called to a dual fidelity: fidelity to the core content of the gospel and fidelity to the primary context of a believing community. Whether we are thinking about evangelism, social involvement, pastoral care, apologetics, discipleship, or teaching, the content is consistently the Christian gospel, and the context is consistently the Christian community. What we do is always defined by the gospel, and the context is always our belonging in the church. Our identity as Christians is defined by the gospel and the community.

Being gospel-centered actually involves two things. First, it means being word-centered because the gospel is a word—the gospel is news, a message. Second, it means being mission-centered because the gospel is a word to be proclaimed—the gospel is good news, a missionary message.

So maybe we really have three principles. Christian practice must be (1) gospel-centered in the sense of being word-centered, (2) gospel-centered in the sense of being mission-centered, and (3) community-centered.

1. gospel-centered { 1a. word-centered

1b. mission-centered

2. community-centered

You may think this sounds like a statement of the obvious. We hope you do. But let us make two points by way of introduction.

1. In practice, conservative evangelicals place a proper emphasis on the gospel or on the word. Meanwhile others, like those who belong to the so-called emerging church, emphasize the importance of community. The emerging church is a loose movement of people who are exploring new forms of church. Each group suspects the other is weak where it is strong. Conservatives worry that the emerging church is soft on truth, too influenced by postmodernism. The emerging church accuses traditional churches of being too institutional, too program-oriented, often loveless and sometimes harsh.

Let us as authors nail our colors to the mast from the outset. We agree with the conservatives that the emerging church is too often soft on truth. But we do not think the answer is to be suspicious of community. Indeed, we think that conservatives often do not "do truth" well because they neglect community. Because people are not sharing their lives, truth is not applied and lived out.

We also agree with the emerging church movement that conservative evangelicals are often bad at community. The emerging church is a broad category and an "emerging" one at that, with no agreed-upon theology or methodology. This means that generalizations about the emerging church are far from straightforward. But many within the movement seem to downplay the central importance of objective, divinely revealed, absolute truth. This may not be a hard conviction, but it is a trajectory. Others argue that more visual media (images, symbols, alternative worship) should complement or replace an emphasis on the word. We do not think this is the answer. Indeed, we think emerging church can sometimes be bad at community because it neglects the truth. If Christian community is not governed by truth as it should be, it can be whimsical or indulgent. There is a danger of community becoming me and my acquaintances talking about God—church for the *Friends* generation—middle-class twenty- and thirty-somethings' church. This certainly is not true of all that calls itself emerging church, but it is a danger. Only the truth of the gospel reaches across barriers of age, race, and class.

We often meet people reacting against an experience of conservative churches that has been institutional, inauthentic, and rigidly programmed. For them the emerging church appears to be the only other option. We meet people within more traditional churches who recognize the need for change but fear the relativism they see in the emerging church. For them existing models seem to be the only option. We also meet people within the emerging church movement who want to "do church" in a different way but do not want to buy into postmodern or post-evangelical notions of truth.

We believe there is an alternative. We need to be enthusiastic about truth and mission *and* we need to be enthusiastic about relationships and community.

2. Rigorously applying these principles has the potential to lead to some fundamental and thoroughgoing changes in the way we do church. The theology that matters is not the theology we profess but the theology we practice. As John Stott says, "Our static, inflexible, self-centered structures are 'heretical structures' because they embody a heretical doctrine of the church." If "our structure has become an end in itself, not a means of saving the world," it is "a heretical structure."[1]

Being both gospel-centered and community-centered might mean:

- seeing church as an identity instead of a responsibility to be juggled alongside other commitments
- celebrating ordinary life as the context in which the word of God is proclaimed with "God-talk" as a normal feature of everyday conversation
- running fewer evangelistic events, youth clubs, and social projects and spending more time sharing our lives with unbelievers
- starting new congregations instead of growing existing ones
- preparing Bible talks with other people instead of just studying alone at a desk
- adopting a 24-7 approach to mission and pastoral care instead of starting ministry programs
- switching the emphasis from Bible teaching to Bible learning and action
- spending more time with people on the margins of society
- learning to disciple one another—and to be discipled—day by day
- having churches that are messy instead of churches that pretend

We have called this book *Total Church*. Church is not a meeting you attend or a place you enter. It is an identity that is ours in Christ. It is an identity that shapes the whole of life so that life and mission become "total church."

Is this "gospel plus" (requiring something—in this case, Christian community—in addition to the gospel, which thereby robs the gospel of its saving power)? The answer is, it depends how you tell the gospel story. It depends whether you see the gospel simply as the story of God saving individuals or as the story of God creating a new humanity.

Part 1, "Gospel and Community in Principle," outlines the biblical case for making gospel and community central principles for Christian life and mission. Part 2, "Gospel and Community in Practice," applies this double focus to various areas of church life. Activists may be tempted to skip Part 1 and go straight to Part 2, but the applications in Part 2 are integrally linked to the convictions outlined in Part 1. We are trying to do more than assemble a collection of "good ideas" for church life. We have tried to explore the contemporary implications of the preoccupation with the gospel word and gospel community in the Bible story.

WHO WE ARE

It might be helpful to include a brief word about the ministry in which we, Steve and Tim, are involved. The Crowded House is a network of missionary congregations, most of which meet in homes. We are trying to "do church" in a way that is welcoming for unchurched people. We place a big emphasis on sharing our lives with one another and welcoming unbelievers into the network of relationships that make up the church. It also means we grow by planting new congregations rather than acquiring bigger premises.

This book, however, is not an argument for household church. Not all our congregations meet in homes. It is our conviction that the principles we outline can and should be applied to all congregations. Nor is this book an account of The Crowded House. We do not think the way we do mission and church is the "right way" or the "only way." It is not an off-the-shelf model that people can fit to their context without alterations. Most of what we say in the book is what we aspire to, but sadly not yet what we do! It is a book of principles, vision, and hopes, not a description of practice.

Where we have included stories, we are seeking to encourage readers to respond imaginatively. We often find that people conceive principles simply in terms of their current practice. At the other extreme, some people see such a vast gulf between principles and current practice that they think the pursuit of principles is futile. This failure of imagination can prevent us from applying the Bible as we should. We hear it speak to us but either find it too far removed from current experience to feel it possible or squeeze it into our current experience. We need Spirit-inspired imagination to reconfigure church and mission around the gospel word and the gospel community.

We have written this book together and so generally used plural pronouns (we, us). But where we describe an experience or story particular to one of us, we have used a singular pronoun (I, me).

part ONE

Gospel and Community
in Principle

WHY GOSPEL?

"PROVE THERE'S A GOD—that's all we ask," we might say. Philip said to Jesus, "Show us the Father and that will be enough for us" (John 14:8). Philip wanted a vision of God, a spiritual experience, a display of glory, an act of power. What he got was a man talking, for Jesus said in response, "Anyone who has seen me has seen the Father." God is revealed in the person of Jesus and "the words I say to you" (vv. 9–10).

People today want a vision of the divine or proof that God exists or to know the meaning of life or just a sense of purpose. Some want spiritual experiences or acts of power. Some Christians think rational apologetic arguments are the way to persuade people. Others believe the church needs to perform miraculous signs. But today God is still known through "the words I say to you."

Jesus continued, "The words I say to you are not just my own. Rather, it is the Father, living in me, who is doing his work" (v. 10). We expect Jesus to say, "Through the words I say, the Father is speaking his words." But he goes further. Through the words of Jesus, the Father is doing his work. And God is at work today through the proclamation of the gospel. The works of Jesus can be done by every Christian: "Whoever believes in me will also do the *works* that I do; and greater *works* than these he will do, because I am going to the Father" (v. 12 ESV). God will do his work as we proclaim the word of Jesus. The "greater works" are not flashier miracles as if we regularly ought to be outperforming the raising of Lazarus from the dead! John has already defined those "greater works": ". . . greater works than these will he show him, so that you may marvel. For as the Father raises the dead and gives them life, so also the Son gives life to whom he will. . . . Truly, truly, I say to you, whoever hears my word and believes him who sent me has eternal life" (John 5:20–24 ESV; see also 6:29–30). The greater work is to bring people to eternal life through our proclamation of the gospel.

Imagine you are teaching the Bible to a group of young teenagers. Most of them are not taking a bit of notice. You have worked hard to be both true to the text and relevant to the youngsters. But they are just flicking bits of paper at each other. It might be tempting to play some games to show that Christians can have fun too or to sing more songs so they will encounter God in the music. It is in moments like these that we need to hold on to the conviction that God is known and God works through the words of Jesus. Christian ministry must be gospel-centered.

As we stick at the task of proclaiming the gospel, Jesus gives us a lovely promise: "I will do whatever you ask in my name, so that the Son may bring glory to the Father" (John 14:13). In John's Gospel the Father is glorified as the Son gives eternal life (John 17:1–5)—the "greater work" Jesus promises to do through our words (John 5:20–24). When we pray, Jesus promises to do the greater work of giving life in his name—the name we proclaim in the gospel.

GOD RULES THROUGH HIS WORD

Christianity is word-centered because God rules through his gospel word. When Jesus taught in John 14 that God does his work through his word, he was reflecting the common principle of the story of salvation.

In the beginning, when the earth was formless and empty, God *said*, "Let there be light" and there was light (Genesis 1:1–3).

Through his word he brought order out of chaos and light out of darkness (John 1:1–3). Where God's word is not heard, chaos and darkness close in again. When Jeremiah is given a vision of God's coming judgment, he says, "I looked at the earth, and it was formless and empty; and at the heavens, and their light was gone" (Jeremiah 4:23). "Formless and empty" is the same Hebrew expression used in Genesis 1:2 for the chaos and darkness before God's creative word.

Adam and Eve were to express their commitment to God's reign by trusting his word of command not to eat the fruit of the tree. That is why the rejection of God's rule begins with a rejection of God's word. The serpent encourages the woman to doubt God's word (Genesis 3:1) and then to deny God's word (v. 4). Instead the woman is governed by what seems "pleasing to the eye" (v. 6). God rules as his word is trusted and obeyed. God is rejected when his word is not trusted and not obeyed.

When he calls Abraham, God begins his plan to restore his rule and create a new humanity. He speaks a word of promise. He promises Abraham a people who know God, a land of blessing, and blessing to all nations. This is the promise that drives the story of the Bible. When God liberates his people from Egypt, he does so because of his promise to Abraham (Exodus 2:23–25; 3:15; 6:8). Paul calls it the gospel announced in advance (Galatians 3:6–9). A promise is a word about the future, and this future orientation gives God's promise its redemptive character. It is not a statement of what is, but a statement of what will be. The word of promise governs Abraham's action, sending him out from Ur to a life of hopeful pilgrimage. God is reestablishing his rule through his word.

When God liberates his people from Egypt, his word is expressed in the Law given at Mount Sinai. The Law of Moses is given as the word by which God rules his people as they wait for the coming Savior. It is a liberating law, given to bless God's people. It was the lie of the serpent to portray God's rule as harsh and tyrannical. The reality is that the rule of God is a rule of life, blessing, peace, and justice. God rules through his word, and his rule brings freedom and joy. Hence the psalmist's delight in God's Law (Psalm 119:77, 97). Israel had been liberated from the oppressive rule of Pharaoh. God's liberating Law protected from oppression and ensured provision for all. The story of Ruth is a lovely portrait of God's liberating word in action. When people live under God's reign through commitment to his word, Gentile widows are welcomed, protected, and blessed. As God's people lived under his reign through obedience to his word, they would attract the nations to God.

But time and again God's people reject his word. The people ask for a king because they want to be ruled like the nations rather than by God through his word (1 Samuel 8:7). God gives them a king but at the same time raises up prophets to call the people back to his word. The king is to rule under God's rule expressed through his word (Deuteronomy 17:14–20). The prophet is to guide the king so that the king rules under God's authority. That is the ideal. More often, however, the prophet keeps the king in check, calling him back to God's word. Often the word of the prophet and the rule of the king are in conflict.

In the Hebrew canon the history books of the Old Testament (Joshua to 2 Kings) are called the Former Prophets. The main force in these books is not the kings or the international powers, but the word of the Lord that comes by his prophets. God's word is sovereign (see, for example, 1 Kings 13). The book of Deuteronomy promises blessings if the people are faithful to the covenant and curses if they are unfaithful (Deuteronomy 28–30). This is the principle by which the writer of Kings interprets history. What happens to Israel happens because those curses come into play. God's word is sovereign, and so there is something inexorable about the story. The disaster that falls on Israel is a result of the judging and destroying power of God's Law. God's word sets in motion events that cannot be altered.

But the unfaithfulness of God's people cannot sabotage God's gospel word. God does not give up on his promise to Abraham. The prophets not only speak the word of judgment that brings down

Jerusalem by the hand of Nebuchadnezzar—they also speak a word of hope. God promises to send a new king who will reestablish God's liberating rule. That king is Jesus. With a word Jesus heals the sick, and with a word he expels demons (Matthew 8:8, 16). He speaks a word, and people leave all to follow him (Mark 1:14–20). Indeed Jesus is the living Word of God (John 1:1–3). He is both the promised messianic king and the Word by which God rules.

In the life of the believer and in the life of the church God still rules through his word. People become Christians when they respond in faith to the message of the gospel. "I tell you the truth," says Jesus, "whoever hears my word and believes him who sent me has eternal life and will not be condemned; he has crossed over from death to life" (John 5:24; Romans 10:17; Ephesians 1:13; James 1:18; 1 Peter 1:23). The true disciples of Jesus are those who "abide in [his] word" (John 8:31 ESV; Matthew 4:4). It is the holy Scriptures that make Christians "wise for salvation"; that are sufficient for "teaching, rebuking, correcting and training in righteousness" and make us "thoroughly equipped for every good work" (2 Timothy 3:15–17). "The word of God is living and active," says the writer of Hebrews. "Sharper than any double-edged sword, it penetrates even to dividing soul and spirit, joints and marrow; it judges the thoughts and attitudes of the heart" (Hebrews 4:12). It is as if the word of God does laser surgery on our souls. It exposes our thinking and motives. It is the only mirror in which we truly see ourselves, for it is the mirror that reflects our hearts (James 1:22–25).

In John 2 the disciples put their faith in Jesus when they see his first miraculous sign—turning water into wine at the wedding of Cana (v. 11). This story is followed by the cleansing of the temple and Jesus' declaration that *he* is the temple. John comments, "After he was raised from the dead, his disciples recalled what he had said. Then they believed the Scripture and the words that Jesus had spoken" (v. 22). There is a kind of faith that comes from seeing miraculous signs, but true faith comes through the words of Scripture and the words of Jesus. John goes on, "Now while he was in Jerusalem at the Passover Feast, many people saw the miraculous signs he was doing and believed in his name. But Jesus would not entrust himself to them, for he knew all men" (vv. 23–24). Jesus does not trust the kind of faith that comes from seeing miraculous signs. It is not difficult to imagine why. Such faith is likely to be fair-weather faith. It will believe when signs are performed, prayers are answered, things are going well. But it is not the sort of faith that will survive the loss of a child, a period of illness, or some other trauma. Persevering faith comes through the word of God.

In the church the risen Christ rules through his word. This is why the only skill required of church leaders is that they can teach, rightly handling and applying the word of God. Their authority is a mediated authority. They have no authority in and of themselves. Instead they exercise Christ's authority on his behalf as they teach and apply the word. This defines the amazing extent of their authority: when they apply the word they are exercising the authority of God himself. But it also defines the limit of their authority: they have authority only as they teach God's word. They should not exercise an authority that comes because of the position they hold or the force of their personality. It is through their teaching that leaders exercise the authority of Christ, the Head of the church.

GOD EXTENDS HIS RULE THROUGH HIS WORD

Christianity is mission-centered because God extends his rule through his gospel word. The sower in the parable of the sower sows the word (Mark 4:14). The growth of the kingdom comes when people "hear the word" of God and "accept it" (v. 20). Christ's new family is built around those who do God's will (3:35). The new Israel is constituted by the preaching of the gospel (3:14). The kingdom grows when people hear and accept the word of God. For Mark's readers Jesus is gone, ascended into heaven. But Mark reassures them that their king continues to be present through his word.

It is because all authority has been given to him that Jesus sends us to teach all nations (Matthew 28:18–20). It is through the preaching of the gospel that Jesus wields his scepter in the world. To tell people the gospel is to announce the kingdom or kingship of God and his Christ. Through the gospel, we command people to submit to Jesus. Through the gospel, judgment is passed on those who reject him. We are ambassadors of the coming King, going ahead to warn of his coming. If people acknowledge his lordship, they will experience his coming rule as blessing, life, and salvation. If they reject him, they will experience his coming as conquest and judgment.

The book of Acts is structured around summary statements that describe the growth of the church. Often the word of God is the agent of the sentence. "So the word of God spread" (Acts 6:7). "But the word of God continued to increase and spread" (Acts 12:24; 13:49; 19:20). The growth of God's kingdom is synonymous with the spread of God's word. The kingdom grows through the word as it elicits faith.

THE SWORD OF THE SPIRIT

We often divide into word-centered and Spirit-centered churches. For some the key event on Sunday mornings is the sermon; for others it is the "time of worship" or "ministry."

We reject this polarization. Our concern to be word-centered does not conflict with a concern to be Spirit-centered. Churches must be Spirit-centered. The church is the community of the Holy Spirit. It is a living community where things happen because God is at work. When our hearts are moved in worship, when people are changed by God's word, when we turn to God in prayer, when we care for one another, when we act in selfless ways, and supremely when people are saved—all these are signs of the Spirit at work. Paul says that "in [Christ] you too are being built together to become a dwelling in which God lives by his Spirit" (Ephesians 2:22). This is not some theoretical entity, nor the perfected church. This is a real, local congregation with all sorts of problems. The community formed by the gospel for the gospel is the community in which God dwells by his Spirit.

Churches can also polarize between intellectualism (what you think is what matters) or emotionalism (what you feel is what matters). In some churches issues of the heart and emotions have become functionally absent. We acknowledge their importance, but they feature little in our lives. Some of us just do not like to talk about our relationship with the Lord in emotive terms. But we need look no further than the Psalms to see how important emotion is in true faith. The Psalms are God's revelation of how we should respond to God's revelation, and they express the full range of emotions: frustration (Psalm 6), passionate praise (Psalm 9:1–2), anger (Psalm 129), sorrow (Psalm 130), quiet serenity (Psalm 131), and so on. We are to love God with our hearts as well as our heads (Matthew 22:36–37). This is what previous generations called "experiential faith." Churches should be emotional communities—communities in which our faith is felt as well as understood.

It is tempting to stress the need for balance as if what we need is a bit of word and a bit of the Spirit or a bit of intellectualism and a bit of emotion. But this is unhelpful. The truth is that in the Bible word and Spirit always go together.

Both word and Spirit were involved in creation. The world was made by God's word (Hebrews 1:1–3), but the Spirit was also present, brooding over the waters (Genesis 1:2). "By the word of the LORD were the heavens made, their starry host by the breath of his mouth" (Psalm 33:6). It is by his Spirit that God breathes his creative word, and it is by his Spirit that God breathes life into humanity (Genesis 2:7; Job 33:4).

It is the same in the experience of Christians. When Jesus promises to send the Spirit, he says the Spirit "will teach you all things and will remind you of everything I have said to you . . . when he, the Spirit of truth, comes, he will guide you into all truth. He will not speak on his own; he will speak only what he hears, and he will tell you what is yet to come" (John 14:26; 16:13). Notice the emphasis on saying, words, truth, and teaching. It is the Spirit who makes Christ's words known to us, applying them to our lives and making them live. They are not dead words, ancient history, a static set of instructions, or an encyclopedia of belief. Through the Spirit they are the living, life-giving words of God (Ezekiel 37:1–14). The Spirit is the Spirit of truth. "All Scripture is God-breathed," says Paul (2 Timothy 3:16). In both Hebrew and Greek *spirit* and *breath* are the same word. The word of God comes on the breath of God. The word of God is "the sword of the Spirit" (Ephesians 6:17).

Spiritual experience that does not arise from God's word is not Christian experience. Other religions offer spiritual experiences. Concerts and therapy sessions can affect our emotions. Not all that passes for Christian experience is genuine. An authentic experience of the Spirit is an experience in response to the gospel. Through the Spirit the truth touches our hearts, and that truth moves our emotions and affects our wills.

This also means that Bible study and theology that do not lead to love for God and a desire to do his will—to worship, tears, laughter, excitement, or sorrow—have gone terribly wrong. True theology leads to love, mission, and doxology (1 Timothy 1:5, 7, 17). We should not expect an adrenaline rush every time we study God's word. We all express our emotions in different ways. But when we study God's word we should pray that the Spirit of God will not only inform our heads but also inspire our hearts.

Part of our problem is that we often assume an experience of God will be some kind of revelation—a dream, an inner voice, a guiding sense of peace, an encounter, a word. This assumption is reinforced by mysticism and existentialism. But we have no reason to need or expect a revelation from God. God has revealed himself in his Son and in his word. And God's word is wholly adequate and sufficient. But the Bible does lead us to expect other experiences of God through the Holy Spirit—love for God, love for others, assurance, joy, confidence, peace, and so on. Word and Spirit give us a new desire for God (Romans 8:5–9; 14:17; Galatians 5:17).

True Christian experience is experience that arises through the

Spirit from the revelation of God in Jesus contained in the Bible. God rules through his word, and the Spirit applies that word to our lives. The Spirit opens blind eyes to see the truth and melts cold hearts to respond to God's word. The word of God comes in the power of the Spirit (Acts 10:44; 1 Corinthians 2:4; 1 Thessalonians 1:5–6). If we want to see the Spirit of God at work, we must proclaim the word of God.

We might even say that being word-centered is synonymous with being Spirit-centered. The difference is that we cannot control the Spirit. We cannot determine or even predict when and how he will work (John 3:8). Our role is to read, hear, proclaim, teach, and obey the word. The Spirit's role is to do the work of God through that word. Through the Spirit our words become the living word of God (2 Samuel 23:2). And so we center our lives and ministries on the word of God while praying that God's Spirit will do the work of God through that word.

TO SUM UP

The gospel is a word; so the church must be word-centered.

Being gospel-centered has two dimensions. First, it means being word-centered because the gospel is a word. The gospel is good news. It is a message. It is a message that can be summarized in simple gospel outlines or even the three-word confession, "Jesus is Lord." Yet it is also a message that fills the entire Bible. It is the story of salvation from creation to new creation. It is a word that has become incarnate in Jesus Christ. It is this word that brings new life to people and shapes the life of the church.

The gospel is a missionary word; so the church must be mission-centered.

Second, being gospel-centered means being mission-centered, for the gospel is a missionary word. The gospel is *good* news. It is a word to be proclaimed. You cannot be committed to the gospel without being committed to proclaiming that gospel.

IMPLICATIONS

So being gospel-centered means being word-centered and being mission-centered. The church exists both *through* the gospel and *for* the gospel. At one level this is a motherhood-and-apple-pie declaration. Few Christians are going to object to being gospel-centered, just as no one is against mothers or apple pie. The problem is the gap between our rhetoric and the reality of our practice. The continual challenge for us is to apply this principle to church life and ministry without compromise.

A woman once told me about the difficulties she faced as a Brit fitting into American culture. One of her struggles was with people who said, "Let's do lunch." She expected them to phone and arrange a date. They never did. "Let's do lunch" was just an idiomatic way of saying farewell. We all say, "Let's do mission," but does it carry any more intent than "Let's do lunch"?

We sometimes ask people to imagine they are part of a church-planting team in a cross-cultural situation in some other part of the world:

- What criteria would you use to decide where to live?
- How would you approach secular employment?
- What standard of living would you expect as pioneer missionaries?
- What would you spend your time doing?
- What opportunities would you be looking for?
- What would your prayers be like?
- What would you be trying to do with your new friends?
- What kind of team would you want around you?
- How would you conduct your meetings together?

We find it easier to be radical in our thinking when we transplant ourselves outside our current situation. But we are as much missionaries here and now as we would be if we were part of a cross-cultural team in another part of the world. Mission is central to us wherever we are. These are the kind of questions we should be asking wherever we are.

Name: Beth
Occupation: Overseas law student
Church: The Crowded House, Crookes, England

"The Crowded House has made me tear up the script of my life and start again." While she can laugh saying it, Beth's experience of church since arriving in Sheffield from Kenya to study law has been confronting and quite revealing. "When I was asked if I wanted to go to The Crowded House, I went 'The crowded what?' But it's made me go back to square one and start things again with a different motivation."

Beth had her career path pretty much mapped out: study law in the UK before trying her luck as a lawyer in the city, hopefully with a big pay packet at the end of it. That she now sees her future in an advocacy role, or working with a private organization, is testament to the way in which the Christian community she is a part of has challenged her. "When one of our leaders left his job at the bank so he could teach English as a second language, I said, 'What on earth are you doing that for?' Before joining The Crowded House I'd never dreamt someone would do that."

The early times were difficult, as Beth's experience in Kenya was a big church—several thousand people and multiple services. "At first I'd squirm," she says. "When we were so close together my sins seemed so much more apparent to others. Back home if you fell out with someone you could always sit on the other side of the auditorium and never have to see them again." What convinced Beth to stay despite these differences? "It was the friendships," she says. "Eventually I couldn't find a reason to leave."

The ripples from the waves in Beth's life have reached as far as her homeland. Her father, who is not a Christian, is astounded at how caring the Crookes community is to his daughter. Once, when returning to Sheffield late at night following a trip back to Kenya, her father was worried about her getting home safely. When a couple of the leaders offered to pick her up from the station, her dad couldn't believe it. "Now whenever he is on the phone he says to say hello to Pastor Rob and his wife," she laughs. "It's really made him think."

In his book *The Mission of God*, Chris Wright shows that the Bible story is "all about mission"—God's mission to save a people for himself through Jesus Christ. Jesus is the focus of the story, but his identity has missionary implications (Luke 24:45–48). This radical, God-centered perspective, Wright suggests, "turns inside out and upside down some of the common ways in which we are accustomed to think about the Christian life. . . . It constantly forces us to open our eyes to the big picture, rather than shelter in the cosy narcissism of our own small worlds."

- We ask, "Where does God fit into the story of my life?," when the real question is "Where does my little life fit into this great story of God's mission?"
- We want to be driven by a purpose that has been tailored just right for our own individual lives, when we should be seeing the purpose of all life, including our own, wrapped up in the great mission of God for the whole of creation.
- We talk about "applying the Bible to our lives." What would it mean to apply our lives to the Bible instead, assuming the Bible to be the reality—the real story—to which we are called to conform ourselves?
- We wrestle with "making the gospel relevant to the world." But in this story, God is about the business of transforming the world to fit the shape of the gospel.
- We argue about what can legitimately be included in the mission that God expects from the church, when we should ask what kind of church God wants for the whole range of his mission.
- I may wonder what kind of mission God has for me, when I should be asking what kind of me God wants for his mission.[1]

In March 2003, the London Institute for Contemporary Christianity in association with the Evangelical Alliance published a report entitled "Imagine How We Can Reach the UK." It was the result of a major research project involving hundreds of questionnaires and consultations with church leaders. The report concluded: "The reason the UK church is not effective in mission is because we are not making disciples who can live well for Christ in today's culture and engage compellingly with the people they meet. . . . Jesus has a 'train and release' strategy, while overall we have a 'convert and retain' strategy."[2] In the last twenty years, it claimed, we have produced plenty of creative evangelistic materials, but little to help Christians connect their faith to the whole of life. The report blames this on a sacred-secular divide: "the pervasive belief that some things are important to God—such as church, prayer meetings, social action, Alpha—but that other human activities are at best neutral—work, school, college, sport, the arts, leisure, rest, sleep." As a result:

> The vast majority of Christians have not been helped to see that who they are and what they do every day in schools, workplaces or clubs is significant to God, nor that the people they spend time with in those everyday contexts are the people God is calling them to pray for, bless and witness to. So we pray for our Sunday school teachers but not, for example, for schoolteachers working 40 hours a week in schools among children and adults who on the whole don't know Jesus. We pray for overseas missionaries but not for Christian electricians, builders, shop assistants and managers in our towns. . . . We have simply not been envisioned, resourced and supported to share the Good News of Jesus in our everyday contexts.[3]

This is how one of the leaders of The Crowded House put it:

> If someone was being sent as a missionary to a hostile context overseas, our attitude would be something like this: We would expect to pray often for them. We would expect progress in building relationships and sharing the gospel to be slow. We would be excited by small steps—a gospel conversation here, an opportunity to get to know someone there. We would thrive on regular updates from the front line. But the truth is that the lives of many Christians in work, and play, are just like the life of that far-flung missionary! They are lived out in tough environments where progress is often slow and many factors make evangelism extremely difficult. The challenge is to make news from the staff canteen as valued as news from the overseas mission field.

We have a ghetto mentality. We think of church as the faithful few, backs against the wall. But in fact during the week we are dispersed throughout the world. We are already infiltrating the kingdom of Satan. Day by day the people in our churches are rubbing shoulders with unbelievers in their workplaces, schools, neighborhoods, and clubs. We are yeast in the dough (Matthew 13:33). The "Imagine" report concluded: "The UK will never be reached until we create open, authentic, learning and praying communities that are focused on making whole-life disciples who live and share the Gospel wherever they relate to people in their daily lives."[4]

The challenge for us is to make the gospel the center of our lives not just on Sunday mornings but on Monday mornings. This means ending distinctions between "full-timers," "part-timers," and people with secular employment in our team and leadership structures. We need non-full-time leaders who can model whole-life, gospel-centered, missional living. It means thinking of our workplaces, homes, and neighborhoods as the location of mission. We need to plan and pray for gospel relationships. This means creating church cultures in which we see normal, celebrating day-to-day gospel living in the secular world and discussions of how we can use our daily routines for the gospel.

2

WHY COMMUNITY?

PAUL EMPHASIZES HERE, and in many other places, that Christ wants to create 'a people,' not merely isolated individuals who believe in him."[1] So says Sinclair Ferguson, the Scottish pastor and theologian, commenting on Titus 2:14. We are not saved individually and then choose to join the church as if it were some club or support group. Christ died for his people, and we are saved when by faith we become part of the people for whom Christ died. The story of the Bible is the story of God fulfilling the promise, "I will take you as my own people, and I will be your God" (Exodus 6:7; Revelation 21:3). If the gospel is to be at the heart of church life and mission, it is equally true that the church is to be at the heart of gospel life and mission. John Stott says:

> The church lies at the very center of the eternal purpose of God. It is not a divine afterthought. It is not an accident of history. On the contrary, the church is God's new community. For his purpose, conceived in a past eternity, being worked out in history, and to be perfected in a future eternity, is not just to save isolated individuals and so perpetuate our loneliness, but rather to build his church, that is, to call out of the world a people for his own glory.[2]

THE CHRISTIAN COMMUNITY IS CENTRAL TO CHRISTIAN IDENTITY

In much of the world the question "Who am I?" is answered communally. According to a Xhosa proverb, "A person is a person through persons." Singaporean, Malaysian, Hong Kong, Cambodian, Australian, and mainland Chinese all proclaim the *tong xiang* or "familyness" that binds them together. For many Muslims membership in the global Islamic community or *ummah* confers identity and demands loyalty. Common to these cultures is the perception that the wider society determines your identity. For most Westerners, however, this starting point feels increasingly strange. We see ourselves less in terms of role identities such as positions held or group affiliations and more in terms of dispositional identities such as character traits or behavioral tendencies. "Who am I?" is becoming a question for which I am encouraged to find, or create, an answer for myself.

An identity that I construct for myself is far removed from an identity I receive by grace. Churches are full of people trying to earn their identity or prove their worth. As a result we lack assurance or contentment or put others down to bolster our own self-perception or are dependent on the approval of others or are self-righteous or vulnerable to any circumstance that prevents us from fulfilling our ministry. But the key defining relationship for Christians is our relationship with God. Who am I? I am a child of God, the bride of his Son, and the dwelling place of his Spirit. And this identity is given to me by grace.

More than that, the Bible shows that we are communal creatures, made to be lovers of God and of others. When it comes to humanity, God does not simply speak a word of command; he engages in conversation. "Let us make man in our image" (Genesis 1:26). This conversation shows that God himself is a social rather than a solitary being. And so his image cannot be borne by an individual, but by man and woman together (Genesis 1:27). Genesis 2 underlines this as the writer tells us that the only thing in all creation that is not good is the man on his own (v. 18). Divine personhood is defined in relational terms. The Father is the Father because he has a Son. God is persons-in-community. Human personhood, too, is defined in relational terms. You can no more have a relationless person than you can have a childless mother or a parentless son. The trinitarian understanding of our humanity suggests we should define ourselves by the network of relationships in which we live: I am a father, husband, church member, child of God. This makes me unique (no one else shares the same matrix of relationships), but it also defines me in relation to other people. I am not autonomous. I am a person-in-community. I cannot be who I am without regard to other people.[3] Into our pervasively individualistic worldview, we speak the gospel message of reconciliation, unity, and identity as the people of God. This is perhaps the most significant "culture gap" that the church has to bridge.

By becoming a Christian, I belong to God and I belong to my brothers and sisters. It is not that I belong to God and then make a decision to join a local church. My being in Christ means being in Christ with those others who are in Christ. This is my identity. This is our identity. To fail to live out our corporate identity in Christ is analogous to the act of adultery: we can be Christian and do it, but it is not what Christians should do. The loyalties of the new community supersede even the loyalties of biology (Matthew 10:34–37; Mark 3:31–35; Luke 11:27–28). If the church is the body of Christ, then we should not live as disembodied Christians.

Peter writes to Christians facing persecution, calling them "*strangers* in the world" (1 Peter 2:11). The word literally means "without family" or "without home" (*paroikos*). The Roman Empire was viewed as a family (*oikos*) with Caesar as its patriarch. But God's people are now outsiders. For many, conversion may also have meant exclusion from their immediate family and its support structures. But the Christians are being built into an alternative "house" (*oikos*) (v. 5). It is not a sectarian ghetto, for it is called to respond to hostility with good works (v. 12), just as Jeremiah told the exiles in Babylon to seek the welfare of the city (Jeremiah 29:7). Nevertheless, the church gives us a new community and a new identity.

Today it is often difficult for people to contemplate conversion to Christ if that means distancing themselves from their existing networks, especially if those are the close bonds of a minority community such as those found in the gay community or among ethnic minorities. They need a new home. In The Crowded House we have also found some people wanting to be part of our church community not initially because they were interested in Christ but because they wanted a kinder, gentler alternative to their existing network of relationships. In one case they did not want to associate with other refugees from their homeland because of its violent and factious culture. In another case they wanted to leave a drug-taking group of friends.

Name: Samuel
Occupation: Part-time TESOL (Teacher of English to Speakers of Other Languages)
Church: The Crowded House, Abbey

"We run an open-door policy in our house," laughs Samuel as we sit around his kitchen table. "And an open-fridge-door policy too!" The former Overseas Missionary Fellowship UK student worker and his wife, Fiona, have a "full-on" life with The Crowded House but are adamant they wouldn't have it any other way.

Also sitting at the table having breakfast is one of their lodgers, a young Kurdish asylum seeker who has been through more so far than many of us experience in a lifetime. "For us, The Crowded House is literally that—having people live with us," says Samuel, "and that's something that allows the friends of our lodgers to interact with our lives too. Often we come down in the morning, and there are a couple of Kurdish refugees sleeping on the living room floor."

Samuel splits his time between leadership of TCH Abbey and four mornings a week teaching English as a second language in a local college. Teaching was an eye-opening experience. It didn't take long for Samuel to realize that many of the sixteen- to nineteen-year-old refugees taking English lessons had very damaged lives. "I saw it as my job to try and create a family in the classroom," he says.

The New Testament word for community is *koinonia*, often translated by the now anemic word "fellowship." *Koinonia* is linked to the words "common," "sharing," and "participation." We are the community of the Holy Spirit (2 Corinthians 13:14) in community with the Son (1 Corinthians 1:9)—sharing our lives (1 Thessalonians 2:8), sharing our property (Acts 4:32), sharing in the gospel (Philippians 1:5; Philemon 6), and sharing in Christ's suffering and glory (2 Corinthians 1:6–7; 1 Peter 4:13.). The collection of money by the Gentile churches for the poverty-stricken church in Jerusalem is an act of *koinonia* (Romans 15:26; 2 Corinthians 9:13). Our community life is celebrated and reinforced in Communion, where we participate (*koinonia*) together in the body and blood of Christ: "Because there is one loaf, we, who are many, are one body, for we all partake of the one loaf"(1 Corinthians 10:16–17).

This image of family extends to his view of the Abbey congregation. Another young Christian from the church also lodges with Samuel and Fiona. "We want to be accountable in our generosity and share our possessions," he reveals, adding, "We also want the people who share our home to share our griefs and our joys, and that's why we live open lives."

Samuel also loves the teaching preparation time he spends with Abbey's other leaders. "It's a community hermeneutic," he says. "We discover things in the text of the Bible we'd never discover on our own." This communal learning extends to the congregational meeting, when the fruits of their labors are brought to the rest of the "family." "Often it becomes an extended, directed conversation," says Samuel. "That's when some of our best teaching occurs."

Samuel and Fiona admit they have made choices that have often bewildered their families. In their own words, they live in an "interesting" neighborhood, with people coming and going all the time. Yet, when asked to sum up how he feels about this, Samuel offers the word "content." "We believe we are living the good life," he says. "We want to offer something that comes from within."

Writing to the Thessalonians, Paul says, "For what is our hope, our joy, or the crown in which we will glory in the presence of our Lord Jesus Christ when he comes? Is it not you?" (1 Thessalonians 2:19). The church at Thessalonica is Paul's investment in the future. His future is bound up with them and their progress in the faith. He will boast on the final day not in what he has done but in what they have done. He has staked his reputation before God on them. He goes on, "For now we really live, since you are standing firm in the Lord" (3:8). The NIV has added the word "really." It is literally: "for now we live." Paul's life now is bound up with the church.

The prevailing view of life today is that of an individual standing on his or her own, heroically juggling various responsibilities—family, friendships, career, leisure, chores, decisions, and money. We could also add social responsibilities like political activities, campaigning organizations, community groups, and school associations.

From time to time the pressures overwhelm us, and we drop one or more of the balls. All too often church becomes one of the balls.

We juggle our responsibilities for church (measured predominantly by attendance at meetings) just as we juggle our responsibilities for work or leisure.

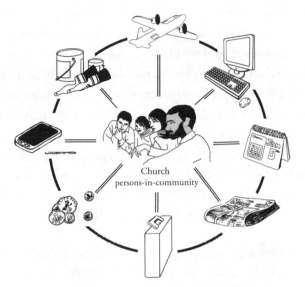

An alternative model is to view our various activities and responsibilities as spokes of a wheel. At the center or hub of life is not me as an individual but us as members of the Christian community. Church is not another ball for me to juggle but that which defines who I am and gives Christlike shape to my life.

According to this model, Bob and Mary do not drop church. Instead, their life as persons-in-community enables them to retain their sanity! For others in the church, some of their engagements (work, leisure, friendships) will adjust for a season as they share responsibility for the new children.

In our experience, people are often enthusiastic about community until it impinges on their decision-making. For all their rhetoric, they still expect to make decisions by themselves for themselves. We assume we are masters of our own lives. "It's my money, it's my life, it's my future," we say, "so it's my decision." In contrast, in The Crowded House we "expect one another to make decisions with regard to the implications for the church and to make significant decisions in consultation with the church."[4] A married man must take into account his wife and family, consulting with them over significant decisions. It should be the same in the family of God. Paul says: "in Christ we who are many form one body, and each member belongs to all the others" (Romans 12:5). My family owns a car. It belongs to us, and so we are responsible for it, and we make decisions about it together. In the same way, in the Christian community we belong to one another, and so we are responsible for one another and make decisions together. This is not a process of "heavy shepherding" where the leader tells people what to do. Our statement does not say decisions are made *for* people. It says they are made *with regard to* the community to which they belong. Nor is it top-down. It is a community process in which everyone is accountable to everyone. As leaders, we submit our schedules, priorities, and key decisions to the community.

Imagine a young couple, Bob and Mary, who are involved in a local congregation. Mary gives birth to twins. Bob and Mary are now facing the prospect of trying to cope with babies who constantly need feeding and changing. In the first model, juggling the church ball alongside the new family responsibilities becomes impossible. Bob and Mary decide they will have to forget being involved in church activities on anything more than a minimal level for quite some time. So they make a unilateral decision to absent themselves from much of church life.

In the alternative model, it is not only Bob and Mary's issue when the babies are born. It is an issue for the whole church. The congregation takes on some of the responsibility because their identity and life is that of persons-in-community. So perhaps a couple of people go around early each morning to bathe the babies so Bob and Mary can have time together over breakfast. Or someone offers to take Bob to work for a few months so that on the way Bob can sleep or read his Bible, or they can pray together because Bob is not getting much chance to do these things at home. Bob and Mary may not be as involved in the church meetings, but they are more involved than ever in the life of the community.

The church is to be a light to the world. Jesus asks us to let that light "shine before men, that they may see your good deeds and praise your Father in heaven" (Matthew 5:16). Church that is a discrete set of responsibilities, juggled among other sets of responsibilities, can never carry the weight of Jesus' mandate. Only life that is infused and transformed by a communal identity can be lived "before men." It is this kind of life that can only be explained in a way that brings praise to our Father in heaven.

> One of The Crowded House congregations has had to adapt to several major changes in recent months. A member from Pakistan has had to start an English course in order to qualify as a nurse on top of her existing job. This means that her husband has taken on more of the care of their young son; so he has less time for his ministry among the Pakistani community. Another couple is expecting their first child, and the husband has just started his own business. One young man moved from part-time work to full-time teacher training while his fiancée started her first full-time job. Rather than expecting church members to adapt to these life changes on their own, others have thought together about what changes it means for them as a church. They have reviewed their meeting times, rethought their gospel opportunities, and shared responsibilities.

THE CHRISTIAN COMMUNITY IS CENTRAL TO CHRISTIAN MISSION

God is a missionary God, and God's primary missionary method is his covenant people. Humanity was made in the image of the Triune God. The purpose of an image is to represent something, and we were made to represent God on earth. God made us as persons-in-community to be the vehicle through which he would reveal his glory. But humanity has grasped for autonomy from God. We fell under the curse of God, and human community has become fractured. The image-bearers of God fall short of his glory.

God begins his plan to create a new humanity with his promise to Abraham. By focusing on Abraham, God has not abandoned the rest of humanity, for through Abraham blessing will come to all nations (Genesis 12:1–3). Although humanity as a whole retains its identity as God's image-bearer, Abraham's family becomes the prism through which God's grace shines to the world. These words of promise set the agenda for the entire biblical story. God fulfils his missionary intent for the nations through the nation of Israel.

After the exodus from Egypt, God constitutes the descendants of Abraham as a nation under his rule. Israel alone is called "out of all nations" as God's "treasured possession" (Exodus 19:4–6). Yet this unique status is good news for the nations. God calls the nation to be "a kingdom of priests." Israel's priests represented God to the people by expounding the Law and represented the people to God through sacrifice and intercession. So the nation as a whole has a priestly role of making God known to the nations and bringing them to the means of atonement. They are also to be "a holy nation." They are set apart by God so God can reflect his character to the nations. The nation was called to live a life of visible holiness in obedience to God's word that would draw the nations to life under God's rule (Deuteronomy 4:6–8).

The tragedy of Israel's history is that instead of drawing the nations to the ways of the Lord, they were drawn to the ways of the nations. The prophets had to keep reminding them of their identity as God's covenant community and of their responsibility to the nations. Isaiah, however, looks beyond the people's unfaithfulness to a day when the nations will stream to "the mountain of the LORD" because they want to live under God's rule and enjoy his blessings (Isaiah 2:2–4). "The fortune of the world ultimately hangs upon the existence of Israel in the midst of the nations; living by Yahweh, the chosen people live for mankind."[5] Israel's mission was essentially centripetal (toward the center). The nation was to be a light to the other nations, drawing them to God's rule as a moth to a flame.

But the nation of Israel failed to live out the implications of her calling. God's glory was smothered under a cloak of disobedience.

The nations looked on in vain, seeing only judgment. But Yahweh will not be frustrated. In Isaiah he promises to raise up a Servant who will be all Israel had been called to be and through whom God will bless all the nations, even as he had promised Abraham. The Servant will be "a light for the nations" so that "my salvation may reach to the end of the earth" (Isaiah 49:6 ESV).

Matthew begins his account of Jesus by describing him as the "the son of Abraham" (Matthew 1:1). Here is the One through whom God will bless all nations. And Matthew ends with Jesus sending his disciples to the nations to bless them through the mission of the church (Matthew 28:18–19). Mission in the Old Testament was centripetal (moving toward the center). Now mission becomes centrifugal (moving away from the center).

But mission does not cease to be centripetal. The attractive covenant community continues to be the means by which God fulfills his promise to Abraham. What has changed is the center! The center is no longer geographic Jerusalem. Now it is the community itself among whom Christ promises to be present (Matthew 28:20). The community moves out across the globe (a centrifugal movement), all the time drawing people to its Lord through its common life (a centripetal movement).

On a mountain and before a watching world, Jesus makes known the word that will govern his community (Matthew 5:1ff.), just as Moses had done for Israel at Mount Sinai. Jesus describes that new community as salt and light (vv. 13–14). Much is made of the properties of salt to preserve and purify. But Jesus did not pluck these metaphors from the air. In the Old Testament salt is used as a symbol of the unbreakable nature of God's covenantal relationship with his people (Leviticus 2:13; Numbers 18:19; 2 Chronicles 13:5). Now Jesus calls his small band of disciples God's new salt community because the old salt community has irreversibly lost its "saltiness." In an overt reference to the judgment of the exile, Jesus refers to the old community being thrown out and trampled underfoot. The new community is also described as "the light of the world" (Matthew 5:14–16). As Israel failed to be a light to the nations, Isaiah promised that the Servant would take on this role. Jesus identifies himself as the fulfillment of this promise (John 8:12). Here Jesus speaks of his messianic community as the light of the world. God's glory will radiate to the nations as they live under the Messiah's rule in obedience to his word. Jesus calls a community into existence and gives it a missional focus with the centripetal force that had been integral to Israel's calling.

The church, then, is not something additional or optional. It is at the very heart of God's purposes. Jesus came to create a people who would model what it means to live under his rule. It would be a glorious outpost of the kingdom of God, an embassy of heaven. This is where the world can see what it means to be truly human.

Our identity as human beings is found in community. Our identity as Christians is found in Christ's new community. And our mission takes place through communities of light. Christianity is "total church."

If you warm to this vision of Christian community, then start where you are. Sell the vision by modeling the vision. Don't become a pain to your existing congregation, telling them everything they are doing is wrong. Become a blessing by offering hospitality, showing practical care, dropping in on people. Create around you a group of Christians who will share their lives and encourage one another in the faith. You might start with your home group. Often home groups are little more than meetings. Make yours a community by acting like a community. You don't have to mount a campaign for change— just get on with it and make community infectious. Create something that other people want to be part of. And think about whether you could establish a context in which people in your church can hang out together and invite unbelieving friends—something like a regular cafe night, an open home, or sports practice.

part TWO

Gospel and Community
in Practice

3

EVANGELISM

John was playing squash with an unbelieving colleague who had recently joined the company. They had had a couple of brief chats over coffee in the cafeteria. Simon was new to the area and so welcomed the chance to do something social, and John seemed to be an "okay sort of bloke." During the game, Simon got hit by a ball and began jumping around the court in pain. Over a drink in the lounge after the game, John and his workmate talked about their match. The incident with the ball was mentioned, and John responded, "It's a hard ball when it comes at that speed. It's happened to me loads. I once knew someone who got it straight in the eye. But have you ever noticed how God seems to play hardball with us in life? It's often far more painful than a squash ball hitting you. Downsizing, bereavement, rejection—the list is endless. How do you respond, Simon, when life hits you like a punch to the kidneys?"

WHAT RESPONSE DOES THIS evangelistic model provoke? Perhaps you are particularly prone to cringe, and John's lead-in line registers high on the scale. Perhaps you find yourself reluctantly admiring his courage and commitment. It is almost impossible to talk about evangelism without people groaning inwardly! Christians whose love for the Lord Jesus flows from new hearts kept soft by the Holy Spirit have an instinctive desire to commend their Savior to others. At the very least, we want to speak of him to those who do not love him because we want God to be honored. The task of evangelism itself, however, is often a different story. Somewhere in the moment, for many of us, the passion evaporates like mist in the morning sun.

Our conviction is that Christians are called to a dual fidelity— fidelity to the core content of the gospel accompanied by fidelity to the primary context of a believing community. To ignore or minimize either is not merely to hamstring the task of evangelism; it is effectively to deconstruct it.

THE GOSPEL WORD IS CENTRAL IN EVANGELISM

Francis of Assisi is alleged to have said, "Preach the gospel always; if necessary use words." That may be a great medieval sound bite, but it falls short of what the Bible teaches about evangelism. Jesus began his public ministry by "proclaiming the good news of God" (Mark 1:14). When he gained a reputation as a miracle-worker, his response was to leave the area so he could give himself to the task of proclamation, for "that is why I have come" (Mark 1:38). And the risen Lord left his disciples with the specific commission to go to the nations, "teaching them to obey everything I have commanded you" (Matthew 28:20).

There is a tendency in some quarters today to promote a kind of evangelism without proclamation. Acts of service are done or people are invited to experience Christian worship. But without words of explanation these are like signposts pointing nowhere or, worse still, signposts pointing to our good works. The gospel is good news—a message to be proclaimed, a truth to be taught, a word to be spoken, and a story to be told.

The message that Jesus proclaimed was, "The kingdom of God is near." And with this message came the call, "Repent and believe the good news!" (Mark 1:15). With the coming of the messianic King, a new age had dawned. Jesus demonstrates the veracity of his proclamation of God's kingship through his words and deeds, culminating in his crucifixion and resurrection. On the cross the King takes upon himself the consequences of our rebellion. As a result, the King graciously commands people to submit in faith and repentance to his lordship so that they might experience his reign of life and freedom. God is at the center of the gospel word. Yet much evangelism tends to place people in that position. The gospel becomes skewed toward me and how Jesus meets my needs. But the gospel Jesus proclaimed is about God exercising his life-giving rule through his Messiah for his glory.

On the squash court John's bold evangelistic effort certainly does not contradict this in terms of its content. In fact, it could be argued that in asserting the sovereignty of God in life, he was announcing the gospel of the kingdom. Legitimate questions remain, however, about John's approach. He hardly knew his colleague. His entry point was strained and tenuous. He had no real idea who his acquaintance was. He made no attempt at building a relationship with him. No questions had been asked of John and no invitation given to him to discuss the big questions of life. John had not earned the right to speak the gospel word to his potential friend.

What if the scenario had gone something like this?

> After the game John and Simon sat in the bar. The conversation was initially a little awkward, but John took a real interest in his colleague—where he had come from and what family he had. It emerged that they had a few things in common, including a shared interest in fast cars. As they were walking out, Simon said, "Would you like to come to a barbecue with me tomorrow night after work?"

THE GOSPEL COMMUNITY IS CENTRAL IN EVANGELISM

The gospel word and the gospel community are closely connected. The word creates and nourishes the community, while the community proclaims and embodies the word. The church is the mother of all believers, Calvin asserted, in that she "brings them to new birth by the Word of God, educates and nourishes them all their life, strengthens them and finally leads them to complete perfection."[1] Martin Luther believed that "The church . . . is constituted by the Word." He also likened the church to a mother "who gives birth to you and bears you through the Word."[2] By her life, created and shaped by the gospel, the church reveals the nature of the inbreaking rule of God. By that gospel life and proclamation, she calls the nations to worship God.

Jesus asserted the centrality of the gospel community in the evangelistic task during his final night on earth. In John 13 he predicts his betrayal. For Jesus it means the hour of his glorification (vv. 31–32). For the disciples it means new responsibilities, and their primary responsibility is to love one another (vv. 34–35). At this crucial moment in the purposes of God, Jesus is concerned for the mutual love of these people. This must mean that love is crucial! Jesus' exhortation is not vague. He turns their attention once more to his own example (vv. 1, 14–17). They are to love in the same way and to the same extent that he has loved them. And the gauge of that love will prove to be the cross.

What is the purpose of this mutual, self-giving love? Don Carson says:

> The new command is not only the obligation of the new community to respond to the God who has loved them and set them free by the offering of his Son. Neither is it merely their response to his gracious choice of them as his people. It is a privilege, which when rightly lived out, proclaims the true God before a watching world. That is why Jesus ends his injunction with the words: All men will know you are my disciples if you love one another."[3]

Before they are preachers, leaders, or church planters, the disciples are to be lovers! This is the test of whether or not they have known Jesus.

That remains the case today: this cross-love is the primary, dynamic test of whether or not we have understood the gospel word and experienced its power. Not our doctrinal orthodoxy, as important as that is. Not our ingenious strategizing, as fascinating as that is. Not our commitment to preaching, as vital as that is. Not our innovative approach to planting, as radical as that may be. It is our cross-love for each other that proclaims the truth of the gospel to a watching and skeptical world. Our love for one another, to the extent that it imitates and conforms to the cross-love of Jesus for us, is evangelistic.

In the alternative scenario for John and Simon, John was treating Simon like a person and taking a genuine interest in his colleague. Although John would have wanted Simon to hear about Jesus, his commitment to him was not dependent upon his readiness to listen to the gospel word. In that way, John was imitating Jesus who responded to people as people, treating them according to their circumstances.

In 1 Thessalonians 2 Paul describes his ministry among the Thessalonians: "We loved you so much that we were delighted to share with you not only the gospel of God but our lives as well, because you had become so dear to us" (v. 8). We can identify forms of evangelism that involve sharing God's word without sharing our lives—some forms of door-to-door and street work, for example. We can also think of sharing our lives without ever having the courage to share God's word. Paul's ministry involved both—sharing his life and sharing the word of God.

> Matt rang to ask what he should do. His friend George had asked him to go street preaching. Matt wasn't interested but didn't know how to respond. So the three of us got together. As the conversation began, it was clear that George thought we were selling out in some way. But as we talked about sharing our lives with unbelievers, about evangelism that was 24/7, about opening our homes, George's tone changed. At the end of our conversation he admitted, "I'm not sure if I'm up for that kind of commitment."

People want a form of evangelism they can stick in their schedule, switch off, and leave behind when they go home. Jesus calls us to a lifestyle of love. Yet the new command of Jesus suggests that whatever advances John made in the second scenario, there is a further vital dimension.

> As they were walking out, Simon said, "Would you like to come over for a barbecue tomorrow night after work?" "Sorry, I can't," said John, "but you could come to ours. We already have a few friends coming over, and it would be great if you came too." Simon hesitated. "I wouldn't want to intrude," he said. "Also I'd feel a bit awkward—I don't know anyone. Some other time maybe." "Guess so," said John, "but I know a couple of my friends are bringing their friends I don't know. It's just the kind of thing we do!" Simon smiled. "What the heck, you only live once! I'll bring a bottle."

Ideally evangelism is not something to be undertaken in isolation. Of course, if opportunity presents itself, the gospel word should be spoken clearly and sensitively in conscious dependence upon the Holy Spirit—whenever, wherever, and to whomever. But evangelism is *best* done out of the context of a gospel community whose corporate life demonstrates the reality of the word that gave her life.

Christian community is a vital part of Christian mission. Mission takes place as people see our love for one another. We all know that the gospel is communicated both through the words we say and the lives we live. What Jesus says is that it is the life we live *together* that counts. Jesus prays that those who believe in the gospel "may be brought to complete unity to let the world know that you sent me and have loved them even as you have loved me" (John 17:20–23). The world will know that Jesus is the Son of God sent by God to be Savior of the world through the community of believers. "No one has ever seen God," says John in his Gospel, "but God the One and Only, who is at the Father's side, has made him known" (John 1:18). The invisible God is made visible through the Son of God. "No one has ever seen God," says John again in his first letter, "but if we love one another, God lives in us and his love is made complete in us" (1 John 4:12). The invisible God is made visible through the love of the people of God. The life of the Christian community is part of the way by which the gospel is communicated. Lesslie Newbigin describes the local congregation as "the hermeneutic of the gospel"—the way in which people understand the gospel.[4]

We need to be communities of love. And we need to be *seen* to be communities of love. People need to encounter the church as a network of relationships rather than a meeting you attend or a place you enter. Mission must involve not only contact between unbelievers and individual Christians, but between unbelievers and the Christian community. We want to build relationships with unbelievers. But we also need to introduce people to the network of relationships that make up that believing community so they can see Christian community in action.

In our experience people are often attracted to the Christian community before they are attracted to the Christian message. If a believing community is a persuasive apologetic for the gospel, then people need to be included to see that apologetic at work. People often tell me how they have tried telling their unbelieving friends about Jesus, but they do not seem interested. So they want to know what to do next. My answer is to find ways of introducing them to the Christian community. The life of the Christian community provokes a response. When Peter says "Always be prepared to give an answer to everyone who asks you to give the reason for the hope that you have," he is not speaking to individuals but to churches (1 Peter 3:15). Too much evangelism is an attempt to answer questions people are not asking. Let them experience the life of the Christian community. The church is the home in which God dwells by his Spirit (Ephesians 2:22). Its life is the life of the Spirit, and its community is the community of the Spirit. Let our relationships provoke questions. And do not worry if your church life is sometimes less perfect than it should be! We do not witness to good works but to the grace of God. Our commitment to one another despite our differences and our grace toward one another's failures are more eloquent testimony to the grace of God than any pretense at perfection.

> Al and Lyssa met when they both volunteered in a local thrift store. Al had grown up in a non-Christian home and was indifferent to Christianity. But when Lyssa invited him to a games night in their home, he readily agreed. It was Al's first introduction to our Christian community. He came a few times, attended church on one occasion, and then stopped. A year or so later someone bumped into Al and invited him along. He became a regular at the games night. He started joining in with other things we were doing as community. He had long since stopped being just "Lyssa's friend"—he had got to know us all. He started asking questions, attending church, and coming to Bible studies. Six months later he was baptized.

I recently received the following email:

I was talking with a Chinese non-Christian yesterday. He told how he'd done a Bible course when he first came to the UK, but had understood almost none of it. A year later, he now wants to study the Bible. He told me it's because he's seen the lives we live and the decisions we make. He commented that everywhere else, in China and in the UK, people try to find happiness in money. But he's noticed that we aren't chasing those things. We don't work all hours for money and possessions. We don't find our identity in our jobs and careers like so many people he knows back home in China. I was able to give up my job in the bank [to have more time for ministry], something he says most people in China would find unbelievable. So he has concluded that this is real happiness and he wants to know about it. Next week we'll start going through the Bible story together.

THE THREE STRANDS OF EVANGELISM

In our evangelism we have developed a simple model to encapsulate these convictions:

Building relationships

Sharing the gospel

Introducing
people to community

Like three strands of a piece of rope, our approach to mission should involve these three elements.

Think about the people you are trying to reach with the gospel or would like to start reaching. Identify ideas (often very ordinary ideas) for building relationships with them, sharing the gospel message, *and* introducing them to the network of believing relationships. Introductions might involve nothing more sophisticated than inviting both Christian and non-Christian friends for a meal or an evening out. It is not enough to build a relationship between one believer and one unbeliever.

When considering this model, it is important to avoid imposing a supposed logical sequence. Often people ask which comes first— introducing people to community, sharing the gospel, or building relationships. None need be the first; nor need progress be made in one area before you can move into one of the others. In reality, any one of the three can occur first, and all three can sometimes begin to happen simultaneously. If one strand is missing, then, in God's sovereign plan, the rope can still hold. But it is stronger when all three are present.

A COMMUNITY PROJECT

So often the call to evangelism produces guilt and despondency. This is due in part to ungodly attitudes such as pride and the fear of man. Paul is clear in 1 Corinthians that we have a "foolish" message to proclaim in a foolish manner (1:18–2:5). So evangelism often makes us look foolish, and few people relish that prospect.

However, not all of us are eloquent or engaging. Not everyone can think on their feet. Some people are simply not good at speaking to strangers and forming new friendships. One of the practical benefits of the three-strand model of evangelism is that it gives a role to all of God's people. By making evangelism a community project, it also takes seriously the sovereign work of the Holy Spirit in distributing a variety of gifts among his people. Everyone has a part to play—the new Christian, the introvert, the extrovert, the eloquent, the stuttering, the intelligent, the awkward. I may be the one who has begun to build a relationship with my neighbor, but in introducing him to community, it is someone else who shares the gospel with him. That is not only legitimate—it is positively thrilling! Pete may never share the gospel verbally with Duncan, but his welcome and love are an integral part of the evangelistic process and should be honored as such. Meanwhile Susan can make friends and introduce them to the community, confident that others will present them—at an appropriate point in an appropriate way—with the challenges of the gospel. It is lovely to think of us making up for one another's deficiencies with our collective community strengths.

If evangelism is a community project, our different gifts and personalities can complement one another. Some people are good at building relationships with new people. Some are socialites—the ones who will organize a trip or an activity. Some people are great at hospitality. Some are good at initiating gospel conversations. Some are good at confronting heart issues. In each case I can think of individuals in our small congregation who fit the bill. I am not good at any of these things. I was the one who did evangelistic Bible studies with Al. At the end I said, "You ought to be baptized," and he said, "Okay." Simple as that! But I would never have got that far if I had not been part of a team.

> Simon walked a little nervously around the back of the house and into the garden. He was glad to find that only a handful of people had arrived and looked around for John. A relieved grin spread over his face as he heard John's voice. "Simon, great to see you. Hey, everyone, this is Simon. Ask him to show you the bruise on the back of his leg!"
>
> It wasn't too long into the evening before Simon realized that quite a few were Christians. He'd never known so many, but they seemed okay. He was actually enjoying the evening and wasn't opposed to watching the game with them on the weekend when they suggested it. He struggled to put his finger on it, but there was a sort of underlying gentleness in the way they related. He hadn't experienced it before. "Cool," he found himself thinking, though he wasn't at all sure what to make of the conversation about Jesus.

ORDINARY LIFE, GOSPEL INTENTIONALITY

Major events have a role to play in church life, but the bedrock of gospel ministry is low-key, ordinary, day-to-day work that often goes unseen. Most gospel ministry involves *ordinary people doing ordinary things* with gospel intentionality. Whether it is helping a friend, working at the office, or going to the movies, there is a commitment to building relationships, modeling the Christian faith, and talking about the gospel as a natural part of conversation. People often ask if they can come to see our ministry at The Crowded House. But all there is to see is ordinary people doing ordinary things. There are no projects, no programs, no "ministries."

But the "ordinary" is only a vehicle for Christian mission if there is *gospel intentionality*. The ordinary needs to be saturated with a commitment to living and proclaiming the gospel. The gospel is a message, and so mission only takes place as we share that word with people. A commitment to mission through community works only if the priority of the gospel is a strong value within that community. Otherwise we simply form good relationships that never go anywhere. We may even hesitate to share the gospel for fear of jeopardizing those relationships. We fear that if we talk about Jesus, people will not want to be our friends, and the relationship will be broken. Indeed that may happen. And so we need to have the priority of the gospel clear in our minds. This does not mean ramming it down people's throats at the first opportunity. It does, however, mean aiming clearly to reach the point where we can open the Bible with people.

In a poor area of our city there is a Christian coffee shop. Whenever I walk past, it is all but empty. A few doors down is a Kurdish restaurant. Up some treacherous stairs at the back is a smoked-filled game room where Kurdish men hang out. Some Christians have begun frequenting it—drinking tea, playing backgammon, building relationships. Many gospel opportunities have followed. Whether it is projects, cafes, events, or centers, we often assume we need to organize something. For many Christians, especially in smaller churches, this makes evangelism and social involvement seem beyond them. They do not have the resources of time or money required. But there are plenty of opportunities we can join, attend, visit, participate. Often this approach is more effective. We meet people on their territory rather than making them come onto our territory. What this requires is gospel intentionality.

The need for gospel intentionality means that leaders must work hard to create and reinforce this gospel culture. I remember speaking at a conference about ordinary life with gospel intentionality. Questioner after questioner asked me about the structures that needed to be in place. But you cannot program ordinary life! "When do you do evangelism?" people asked. "When do you pastor one another?" "While I do the washing up" did not seem to satisfy them, but it was the only answer I could give! All this requires people who are proactively committed to speaking the gospel to unbelievers (and other Christians). We try to create this culture by regularly teaching our values, celebrating gospel opportunities, setting aside time each Sunday to share what we have been doing, "commissioning" people as missionaries in their workplaces and social clubs. Above all we model the culture for one another so that it becomes the normal thing to do. We need Christian communities who saturate ordinary life with the gospel. The communities to which we introduce people must be communities in which "Godtalk" is normal. This means talking about what we are reading in the Bible, praying together whenever we share needs, delighting together in the gospel, and sharing our spiritual struggles, not only with Christians but with unbelievers.

We want our life together to be gospel-saturated. We want to live and talk the gospel as part of our shared life. At the same time we try to make our meetings less strange to unbelievers. We work hard to ensure that everything we do is explained. We want unbelievers to feel comfortable. We want meetings to feel more like family gatherings than religious services. The result is that when people come to a meeting, it is not a big culture shock. They experience something similar to what they have already experienced in the life of the community. At the same time, because we have introduced them to the network of believing relationships, they already know half the people. It becomes a much less threatening occasion.

For six months Fiona had been trying to get one of her housemates to come to church. Luke was reluctant to come to a church "meeting," but he got involved in the community in other ways—going to the movies, watching football in the pub, sharing meals, jogging, and mountain biking. When eventually he first came to a meeting, Fiona wasn't even there. But he already knew 90 percent of the church. What he experienced was not all that different from what he had done with them before except that they sang some songs and studied the Bible. Luke is now a Christian.

Western culture has become very compartmentalized. We divide our lives into work time, leisure time, family time, church time, and mission or outreach time. We want to spend more time in evangelism, but because this can happen only at the expense of something else, it never happens. Rethinking evangelism as relationships rather than events radically changes this. Evangelism is not an activity to be squeezed into our busy schedules. It becomes an intention that we carry with us throughout our day. The same is true of church. If church and mission are redefined in relational terms, then work, leisure, and family time can all be viewed as gospel activities. Ordinary life becomes pastoral and missional if we have gospel intentionality. Watching a film with friends or looking after a burdened mother's children can simultaneously be family time, leisure, mission, and church.

AUTHENTICATING THE GOSPEL

The validity of this three-strand model does not need to be argued for purely on pragmatic grounds. Its primary value is the way it takes the corporate dimension of evangelism seriously. Historically, evangelicals have been so committed to the centrality of the gospel word in evangelism that they can be uneasy about "conceding" the centrality of the gospel community. Talk of the gospel community authenticating the gospel word creates a certain amount of unease. But this is precisely how the Bible describes the people of God.

In Ephesians Paul describes the mystery of the gospel that has been entrusted to him. This mystery is that, through the gospel, Gentiles are included with Jews in God's covenant community (2:14–16; 3:6). Paul goes on, "[God's] intent was that now, through the church, the manifold wisdom of God should be made known to the rulers and authorities in the heavenly realms, according to his eternal purpose which he accomplished in Christ Jesus our Lord" (3:10–11). The Christian community makes God's wisdom known in the heavenly realms. And that is because we are the beginning of God's purposes for the whole cosmos. God is going to bring "things in heaven and on earth together under one head, even Christ"

(1:10). "He chose to give us birth through the word of truth," says James, "that we might be a kind of firstfruits of all he created" (James 1:18). We are the first ray of light breaking through into the darkness of a disordered and fractured universe. We are the first sign of a new dawn. The night of Satan's reign is fading. In C. S. Lewis's vivid imagery, the snows of the White Witch's winter are melting in Narnia. The church is an outpost of heaven. We are heaven on earth. John Stott says:

> The 'mystery' was not an abstraction. It was taking shape before people's eyes. And in this new phenomenon, this new multi-racial humanity, the wisdom of God was being displayed. Indeed the coming into existence of the church as a community of saved and reconciled people is at one and the same time a public demonstration of God's power, grace and wisdom: first of his mighty resurrection power (1:19–2:6), next of his immeasurable grace and kindness (2:7), and now of his manifold wisdom (3:10).[5]

The Holy Spirit brings the church into existence through the gospel word. Through that same gospel word he continues to change people so that they become less lovers of self and more lovers of God and others. This is the community life that models the gospel because it is the life for which we were made. As non-Christians are exposed to this dynamic, they begin to see that the gospel word is more than a set of propositions to be assented to. They see it as the very power of God for healing and wholeness, as the word that brings life and blessing.

In view of contemporary culture, we should not underestimate the need for authenticity among the people of God. Perhaps this need is greater than when cultures are being introduced to Christianity for the first time. The Western world has advantages from a Christian influence stretching back hundreds of years. But this longevity has also brought disadvantages, including a lack of credibility. People have rejected the gospel word in part because they have not been exposed to credible gospel community. Churches have often stood aloof from society. Evangelicals have tended to run away from marginalized urban areas to populate more comfortable suburbs. Christians are often perceived as irrelevant and self-righteous. If these perceptions have any basis, we should not point the finger too quickly at people's spiritual blindness. Jesus gives the world the right to judge the sincerity of our profession on the basis of our love for each other. In other words, we should face with humility the challenge of unbelief. Our response should be one of repentance and faith resulting in lives of authentic corporate existence lived boldly before a skeptical and apathetic world.

> John was pleased to hear Simon's voice at the other end of the phone. He was even more pleased to learn that Simon had spent the previous day with people from church. But even that didn't prepare him for what Simon was about to tell him: "I got into a bit of a heavy conversation with Jake and Tracy. Wasn't sure what to make of it at the start, but their answers to my questions made some sort of sense, I guess. The hardest thing to argue with is the kind of lives you all live. I've never seen anything like it. So, I hope you don't mind, but I've agreed to start looking at the Bible with them for a couple of hours." Mind? John had to keep himself from shouting, "Hallelujah!" Or at least hold it in until he'd put the phone down.

SOCIAL INVOLVEMENT

I WAS TALKING WITH A prominent evangelical church leader and asked him why more people are not open to a household model of church or to community groups meeting in homes. The church leader was candid in his reply: "Because people like me come from professional backgrounds, and we want churches that reflect our backgrounds. I don't want to be opening my home to people. I don't want to get involved in people's lives. I don't want needy people in my church. Before people like me went into Christian ministry, we were lawyers, doctors, businessmen. And when we get involved in ministry we bring those values with us. We want to lead growing churches with professional people, church administrators, healthy budgets. We want church to be a well-run organization with polished presentations."

Dave had spent two years as what is known as a lay assistant and was considering what to do next. He wanted to go into full-time ministry. He has a good grasp of the gospel and is an able communicator. He comes from a working-class background and had worked as a laborer before becoming a lay assistant. He was trying to decide whether to go straight into church planting or complete a theological degree. As he took advice from various people, one prominent evangelical leader told him that he needed a degree so that in future ministry he could relate to doctors, lawyers, and other professionals. Whatever the merits of academic qualifications in preparing for ministry, consider the underlying assumptions behind this advice. While a degree might enable Dave to relate to professionals, it would undoubtedly make him less able to relate to working-class and marginalized people. But the assumption is that "successful" churches are churches with professionals.

A WELCOME FOR THE POOR AND MARGINALIZED

In Luke 4:18–19 Jesus announces his agenda when he reads from Isaiah 61 in the synagogue of Nazareth and claims that these promises are fulfilled in him.

> *"The Spirit of the Lord is on me,*
> *because he has anointed me*
> *to preach good news to the poor.*
> *He has sent me to proclaim freedom for the prisoners*
> *and recovery of sight for the blind,*
> *to release the oppressed,*
> *to proclaim the year of the Lord's favor."*

In 4:35 Jesus "rebuked" (ESV) an evil spirit, freeing a man from its power. And in 4:39 where Jesus "rebuked the fever" in Peter's mother-in-law and "it left her," the word "left" is the same word as "release" in 4:18. Jesus declares that he will "release the oppressed" and then releases those who are oppressed by evil spirits and sickness. It is a sign of his intent, a sign of his coming kingdom.

In Luke 5:27–32 Jesus calls Levi the tax collector and is the guest at a party in his home. The Pharisees and teachers of the Law ask the disciples, "Why do you eat and drink with tax collectors and 'sinners'?" (5:30). In the culture of first-century Palestine, eating was an indication of association and friendship. Indeed, eating continues to function in this way in most cultures of the world. Inviting someone to your home for a meal and accepting such an invitation are both signs of communal bonds. They imply or even create some level of mutual commitment. This is what made Jesus' actions so scandalous to the religious leaders. Eating with tax collectors and sinners was a sign that they could have a place in the community of Jesus. Jesus is proclaiming the coming of the long-expected kingdom of God (4:43). God is at last going to intervene in human history to reestablish his reign. This would mean the vindication of God's people and the judgment of God's enemies. And as far as the Pharisees were concerned, they were clearly in the former group, while the tax collectors and sinners were in the latter. Tax collectors may not have been poor, but they were marginalized. Not only were they notorious for using their power to cheat people, they were collaborators with the Roman occupying force. This made them traitors to the nation and traitors to God. God's Promised Land was defiled by Gentile occupiers, and the tax collectors were on the side of the Gentile defilers. If Jesus is the Messiah, then this means that God sits down to eat with his enemies.

At least that is how it looks to the Pharisees. And Jesus confirms that this is indeed how it is! He responds to their question by saying, "It is not the healthy who need a doctor, but the sick. I have not come to call the righteous, but sinners to repentance" (Luke 5:31–32). Jesus has come for outsiders. He has not come for the sorted-out people but for the broken people ("the poor in spirit") and the messed-up people. He has come to call sinners and welcome them home. God is the God who eats with his enemies. That is the staggering nature of God's gracious character.

The accusation of Luke 5 is repeated in Luke 15: "Now the tax collectors and 'sinners' were all gathering around to hear him. But the Pharisees and the teachers of the law muttered, 'This man welcomes sinners, and eats with them'" (15:1–2). This is the context in which Jesus tells the three great parables of grace in Luke 15—the lost sheep, the lost coin, and the lost son. All three proclaim the amazing grace of God who goes out to look for what is lost. He is the Father who runs to welcome his errant children. But the point of these parables is to show why Jesus eats with the marginalized. At the end of the parable of the lost son, the elder brother is faced with a choice. It is the choice shared by the Pharisees to whom the parables are told and by Luke's readers. We can go to join the party, to accept a kingdom of grace and so associate with sinners, or we can stay outside, cling to a system of merit, and associate only with respectable people.

In Luke 6:20–26 Jesus says that the poor are blessed, for theirs is the kingdom of God. The word *poor* in the Old Testament is used both of the economically needy and the spiritually humble. Luke has both senses in view. The economically needy are a model for those who cry out to God for help (compare 14:12–14 and 14:21), while the faithful people of God find themselves needy because of the world's hostility (6:20–22; 9:57–58). Luke says that those who hunger and who weep are blessed, for they will be filled and will laugh (6:21). Blessed are those who are excluded because of the Son of Man. Meanwhile, he proclaims woe to the rich, the well-fed, those who laugh now and receive the praise of men. This is not because the poor are more saintly—they are sinners like anyone else. Nor is it because Jesus will establish a political kingdom within history. It is because a day of reversals is coming when the first shall be last and the last shall be first (1:51–53; 13:30; 14:11). And this coming kingdom is anticipated in the Christian community—a jubilee community of forgiveness and justice (4:19; 11:4). The marginalized are excluded from the blessings of this life, but the kingdom of God is a kingdom of grace, and so their lack of status, wealth, or power does not exclude them.

John the Baptist announced the imminent coming of God's kingdom, the vindication of God's people, and the judgment of God's enemies (3:9). But when John finds himself languishing in prison, not vindicated and his oppressors not judged, he questions the identity of Jesus. Jesus replies by saying, "Go back and report to John what you have seen and heard: The blind receive sight, the lame walk, those who have leprosy are cured, the deaf hear, the dead are raised, and the good news is preached to the poor" (7:22). Judgment will fall: it will fall vicariously on God's Messiah so that God's enemies can find a home in God's gracious kingdom.

Meanwhile, the sign that Jesus is the Messiah is that good news is preached to the poor.

Jesus' eating with sinners is a wonderful declaration of the riches of God's grace. But notice how this grace plays out in practice. It results in Jesus spending time with the despised and marginalized. It means Jesus has time for the needy. They are his priority. He does not focus on the professional classes, the lawyers, the doctors, the respectable middle classes. Such people are welcomed if they will associate with the ragtag group who make up the community of Jesus—after all, Luke himself is a doctor. But Jesus goes out of his way to welcome the poor, the marginalized, and the needy.

And Jesus expects us to do the same. In Luke 14 he tells the parable of a great banquet. The master of the banquet sends out invitations, but people make their excuses. So he sends his servants out to bring in "the poor, the crippled, the blind and the lame" (v. 21). God graciously invites the spiritually poor, crippled, and blind to his eternal messianic banquet. But this story follows an exchange in which Jesus says, "When you give a luncheon or dinner, do not invite your friends, your brothers or relatives, or your rich neighbors; if you do, they may invite you back and so you will be repaid. But when you give a banquet, invite the poor, the crippled, the lame, the blind" (vv. 12–13). It is the same four categories that are invited to God's banquet. We are to reflect God's grace to us in the way we treat the marginalized. We are not to give high priority to our rich neighbors. Our focus is to be on the poor and needy. Indeed part of our evangelism to the rich is our evangelism to the needy. We subvert their preoccupation with power and success as they see us loving the unlovely. We expose their self-righteousness and selfishness as they see us eating with outcasts. They begin to see Jesus living through us.

As Jesus sees guests jostling for position at a dinner party, he advises them to take lower places at the table so they will be honored when the host moves them to a higher place. "For everyone who exalts himself will be humbled, and he who humbles himself will be exalted" (v. 11). In anticipation of the final day of reversal, we are to humble ourselves by associating with the poor and needy, so that when that day comes we will be exalted by God himself. We will be "repaid at the resurrection of the righteousness" (v. 14).

Luke writes to Theophilus, "so that you may know the certainty of the things you have been taught" (1:4). Theophilus has been taught that, as a testimony to God's grace, a day is coming that will bring history to an end. And this will be a day of reversals in which God will include the marginalized and Gentiles who have faith in his Son and will exclude (judge) the self-important, self-serving, and self-sufficient, exemplified in the religious elite of Israel. The first shall be last, and the last shall be first. This assertion demands evidence if is to be held with "certainty." Luke writes from the conviction that the evidence is to be found in the story of Jesus. Here in the life of Jesus we see the proof of God's ultimate intentions for

Name: Clare
Occupation: Part-time occupational therapist
Church: The Crowded House, Sharrowvale

By her own admission, Clare used to be a lone ranger. Her previous social-action work in a Manchester urban priority area was, she believes, a blend of self-righteousness and individualism. This was challenged when she joined The Crowded House and moved onto Sheffield's own urban priority area—the Manor Park estate—to house-share with other TCH people. Instead of the do-it-yourself attitude that she had nurtured for so long, Clare was confronted with the gospel's call for Christians to live as a mutually accountable community. "I lost the lone-ranger thing," says Clare. "And I found that the Christian community can live radical lives—together."

Along with this came the growing realization that the difficult social problems she was confronting needed more than a band-aid solution. "I had the growing conviction that only the gospel can change the problems that people face in these difficult urban areas," says Clare. This isn't just the gospel in words. "We need to show the Christian lifestyle to those living around us: we need to live in the light of eternity."

humanity. The story of Jesus as it is narrated in the Gospel of Luke gives certainty of this future reality by allowing us to glimpse a foretaste of it in the ministry of Jesus.

Luke wants his readers to believe this word of promise and to put this word into practice by aligning ourselves with the grace of God through the inclusion of the poor. We should, as it were, ensure that we are on the underside of history when the eschatological reversal takes place. The sect of Jesus the Messiah, although now small, persecuted, and marginal, will on the final day be vindicated and glorified. "Blessed is the one who is not offended by me," says Jesus to John, and Luke to Theophilus (7:23 ESV). In the light of the coming reversal, we should adopt a reversal of socioeconomic values. And perhaps the greatest threat to this is the power of money (6:20, 24; 8:14; 12:15–34; 14:33; 16:9, 13–14; 18:24–25).

As well as building relationships on The Manor, Clare works three days a week as a pediatric occupational therapist. "The part-time nature of my work allows me to spend time building community both on The Manor and with my church," she says. "But there are many ways in which my job is relevant to the community. There are plenty of opportunities to plant mums' and toddlers' groups on The Manor, although at the moment it's simply a matter of getting to know people."

While Clare is happy at the Sharrowvale congregation, she cannot wait for The Manor group, currently standing at eight people, to become a fully-fledged church plant. "Eighty percent of Christians live in the top 20 percent of the wealthiest areas in the country," says Clare. "There are big issues on this estate: drugs, crime, families struggling with all sorts of issues. We have to be here for the long-term."

What keeps Clare going in an area that evangelical churches have traditionally abandoned? "Well, for starters, the gospel is true. And then I know that God hears and answers prayer. And finally," she says, bringing the conversation back to where we started, "we always need to make sure that our ministry does not become our idol."

George Watson says, "All societies are unequal . . . but they describe their own inequalities variously." Stein Ringen says, "What is peculiar to Britain is not the reality of the class system and its continuing existence, but class psychology: the preoccupation with class, the belief in class, and the symbols of class in manners, dress and language."[1] The United States, for example, is also an unequal society, and power and wealth mutually reinforce one another. But in Britain social standing is more complex—a combination of wealth, power, and education, reinforced by monarchy, pageantry, and the honors system. And it matters more. The British social system is elitist compared to that of other countries. The upper classes have an inherent confidence in social situations. The lower classes have an inherent inferiority.

This class consciousness runs deep in British evangelicalism. One church leader commented to me recently, "Social class is British evangelicalism's equivalent of racism in American evangelicalism." The failure to renew our social outlook (Romans 12:2) creates mistrust between the classes and races. Individuals are seen as being (or not being) "one of us." I hope this is mostly subconscious. It means the leadership in conservative evangelicalism largely runs along lines of social class. Those from a lower social class who achieve positions of prominence do so by adopting the culture of the upper class. Many of the divisions within evangelicalism in Britain are as much about social class as theological differences. In one direction people are seen as vulgar; in the other direction people are seen as snobbish.

Why does this matter? It matters because we are failing to reach the working class with the gospel. Evangelicalism has become a largely middle-class, professional phenomenon. When we invite people to our dinners and our churches, we invite our friends, our relatives, and our rich neighbors. We do not invite the poor, the crippled, the blind, and the lame. What is at stake is the grace of God.

A WORD FOR THE POOR AND MARGINALIZED

In recent decades evangelism and social involvement have come to be viewed as alternatives or, if not exactly as alternatives, then as separate activities that need to be held in balance. Christians sympathetic to postmodernism see social action positively but are less confident about evangelism, especially evangelism to the poor. They are sensitive to the charge that this might be manipulative. They are rightly put off by situations where help has been conditional on participation in evangelism.

It is striking, then, that Luke's Gospel, which has the most to say about the poor and the inclusion of the marginalized within the Christian community, is also the Gospel that has the most to say about the centrality and sufficiency of God's word.

In Luke 11 a woman says to Jesus, "Blessed is the mother who gave you birth and nursed you" (v. 27). Jesus replies, "Blessed rather are those who hear the word of God and obey it" (v. 28). His true family are "those who hear God's word and put it into practice" (8:21). Jesus tells Martha that "one thing is necessary," and that is the thing Mary chose when she "listened to his teaching" (Luke 10:38–43 ESV). In Luke 11 Jesus responds to the demand for a miraculous sign by saying the only sign that will be given is "the sign of Jonah." In Matthew's Gospel this is a reference to the resurrection. But in Luke it is to Jonah the Preacher. The point is that the Ninevites repented at the preaching of Jonah, but now one greater than Jonah is among them and they will not listen to his message (vv. 29–32).

In Luke 16 Jesus tells the parable of the rich man and Lazarus. It is another parable that links our treatment of the poor with our eternal destiny. But there is an unexpected twist. The rich man asks Abraham to send Lazarus to his five brothers to warn them so they can escape the torment of hell. He suggests that if someone from the dead goes to them, then they will repent. But Abraham replies, "If they do not listen to Moses and the Prophets, they will not be convinced even if someone rises from the dead" (v. 31). "Moses and the Prophets" was a common way of referring to what we now call the Old Testament. The message is that the word of God is sufficient. If people reject the word of God, then even the ghost of a dead person will not persuade them. It is enough to proclaim God's word. How telling, then, that when Someone does come back from the dead, he spends his time teaching the Bible. The Risen Christ spends the first Easter day explaining "Moses and all the Prophets" (Luke 24:25–27, 44–45).

So in any Christian ministry, including ministry among the poor, proclaiming and teaching the word of God must be central. And that is because the greatest need of the poor, as for us all, is to be reconciled to God and so escape his wrath. What makes Christian social involvement distinctly Christian is a commitment to reconciling the poor to God through the proclamation of the gospel.

This means it is never enough to address people's felt needs. Felt needs can be a good point to start because the gospel addresses the human condition in all its complexity. But people do not as a rule express God's judgment as a felt need. People are blind to their true plight. They do not see their greatest need, which is to be reconciled to God through the gospel. If we do not keep people's eternal plight in mind, then immediate needs will force their way to the top of our agenda, and we will betray the gospel and the people we profess to love. The most loving thing we can do for the poor is to proclaim the good news of eternal salvation through Christ. It is by no means the *only* loving thing we can do for them, but it is the *most* loving thing we can do. It would be a crime of monumental proportions knowingly to withhold such good news.

We want to make three assertions about the relationship between evangelism and social action:[2]

1. *Evangelism and social action are distinct activities.*
Good social action is about harnessing the insights and resources of the poor, but the gospel is a message from outside that is addressed to us in our spiritual helplessness and powerlessness.

2. *Proclamation is central.*
Social action without proclamation is like a signpost pointing nowhere. Worse still, it is likely to imply either that salvation is synonymous with socioeconomic betterment or that salvation is through good works like those I am doing.

3. *Evangelism and social action are inseparable.*
People often talk about evangelism being the priority, but this suggests a list of actions that you work through from the top down; if you do not have time for the bottom items (like social involvement), then this does not really matter. But evangelism cannot be separated from social action because mission takes place through relationships, and relationships are multi-faceted. As Paul says of his relationship with the Thessalonians, "We loved you so much that we were delighted to share with you not only the gospel of God but our lives as well, because you had become so dear to us" (1 Thessalonians 2:8).

The thing I desire most for my children is that they might be reconciled to God through the gospel. This desire does not mean I am unconcerned about their temporal needs. I do not simply teach them the Bible. I also try to create a loving home in which they can experience life as blessing. But still my greatest concern is to teach and model the gospel of salvation. It is the same with the poor and marginalized. Love demands that I be concerned for their temporal needs. But the most loving thing I can do for the poor is to tell them they can be reconciled to God through Christ's saving work.

A COMMUNITY FOR THE POOR AND MARGINALIZED

At a poverty hearing organized by Church Action on Poverty, Mrs. Jones, a mother who has lived in poverty all her life, described the experience of poverty like this: "In part it is about having no money, but there is more to poverty than that. It is about being isolated, unsupported, uneducated and unwanted. Poor people want to be included and not just judged and 'rescued' at times of crisis."[3]

In his classic anatomy of poverty Robert Chambers describes poverty as typically composed of a web of five mutually reinforcing factors: lack of resources, physical weakness, isolation, powerlessness, and vulnerability.[4] Poverty is not just lack of resources or physical weakness. Many people suffer these at some point or other in their lives, but they are not poor. Think of a child, for example. Children have no resources and are physically weak. But this does not mean they are poor if they have a family to protect and provide for them. Poverty is also isolation, powerlessness, and vulnerability. It is to be lacking social connections and community.

The Bible commonly uses phrases like "orphans and widows" or "the alien [immigrant]" to speak of the poor (Deuteronomy 10:18–19; Psalm 146:9; James 1:27). Such people represent the poor because they are vulnerable and powerless. They lack husbands, fathers, and kinsfolk to protect and provide for them. The poor are, by definition, those who are powerless and marginal.

Our first instinct when faced with someone in need is to give something to them or do something for them. "Rescuing" the poor, as Mrs. Jones put it, can be appropriate in times of crisis or important as a first step. But if it never moves beyond this, it reinforces the dependency and helplessness at the heart of poverty. The poor remain passive. It does not produce lasting or sustainable change. This is why a central theme of the literature on development is the importance of participation. As a result the development community has created Participatory Reflection and Action (PRA) or Participatory Learning and Action (PLA), a collection of methodologies to facilitate community participation.[5]

But when development professionals talk about participation, they mean participation in projects. It is all about working with the poor to identify their problems, to develop solutions, to monitor progress, to evaluate outcomes. But the poor need more than that. They do not want to participate in projects. They want to participate in *community*. A woman told me, "I know people do a lot to help me. But what I want is someone to be my friend." People do not want to be projects. The poor need a welcome to replace their marginalization; they need inclusion to replace their exclusion; to replace their powerlessness they need a place where they matter. They need community. They need the Christian community. They need the church.

The poor need a friend who will eat and drink with them. In Luke's Gospel, Jesus describes how the religious leaders criticized

John the Baptist because of his fasting. Now they criticize Jesus because of the way he feasts. "The Son of Man came eating and drinking, and you say, 'Here is a glutton and a drunkard, a friend of tax collectors and "sinners"'" (7:34). That is the accusation, and it is true! Jesus *is* the friend of sinners. He eats with them and welcomes them into his community. Luke goes on to tell a story in which a "sinful woman" gatecrashes a party at which Jesus is a guest. She begins to wet the feet of Jesus with her tears, anoint them with perfume, and wipe them with her hair. Make no mistake— this is sexually charged. Only immoral women let their hair down in Jesus' day. What does Jesus do? Nothing. He does not push her away. He does not gently dissuade her. He lets her continue because he sees her love and her faith (7:47, 50). What provokes him into action is not the sin he sees in the heart of the woman, but the sin he sees in the heart of Simon the host. Simon assumes Jesus cannot be a prophet, for he cannot recognize what kind of a woman she is. But the real problem is that Simon cannot recognize the grace of God. Jesus "welcomes sinners and eats with them" (15:2). And he welcomes this woman. Perhaps she was one of the women named by Luke in 8:1–3, included in the community traveling with Jesus, a group that includes Mary Magdalene from whom Jesus had cast seven demons.

The best thing we can do for the poor is offer them a place of welcome and community. Our first priority in social involvement is to be the church, a community of welcome to, and inclusion of, the marginalized. This needs to go deeper than a warm handshake at the door. People are often unaware of how much the culture of their church is shaped by their social class. Someone at the door of a church, for example, may hand a newcomer a hymnbook, Bible, service guide, and bulletin with a smile and greeting without real-izing how intimidating these can be to someone from a nonliterate culture. The social activities to which the poor are invited, the decision-making processes of the church, the unwritten dress codes, the style of teaching can all be alien to the marginalized. As a result, however warm the welcome, the poor can feel marginalized within the church just as they are outside.

The description of Jesus as "a friend of sinners" was an insult or an accusation. It has, of course, become for us a great source of hope. As we recognize our own sinful hearts, we are comforted to know that Jesus is the friend of sinners. God is gracious. But the grace of God meant that Jesus hung out with unrespectable people. People complained about his companions. If our congregations are full of respectable people, then it may be that we have not truly grasped the radical grace of God.

But what about the rich? Are they also needy? Yes. Should we also evangelize them? Yes. The rich have many social needs. More importantly, they, like all classes of people, are "objects of wrath" (Ephesians 2:3). They are "not rich toward God" (Luke 12:21). They need to be reconciled to God through the gospel. And so, yes, we need to evangelize the rich. Indeed this is what Luke's Gospel is about. Doctor Luke is writing as a literate man to Theophilus, another literate man. Both are among the educated elite in Roman society. Luke describes Theophilus as "most excellent" (Luke 1:3). He is probably a man of status. Jesus himself spends time with the rich and powerful, sometimes appealing to them, sometimes challenging them, sometimes provoking them (Luke 11:37–41). But we need to pay attention to Luke's pitch to Theophilus and Jesus' call to the rich within that Gospel. It is not a domesticated, individualistic offer of salvation divorced from the day-to-day realities of life in a fallen world. Luke's call, as we have seen, is for Theophilus to side with the marginalized just as Jesus did. Similarly, Jesus calls on the rich young man to give all for the poor. Jesus identifies this as the idol that enslaves him and prevents him from serving God (18:18–30).

Luke recognizes this is a hard task: that is why he is writing this Gospel. He wants Theophilus to have certainty of the end-time reversal on which he is asking Theophilus to stake his life. He is asking for nothing less than for Theophilus to carry a cross (14:25–27), and he recognizes that this decision requires careful consideration

(14:28–33). This is a lot more than church attendance and personal moral reform, with career, lifestyle, and social attitudes left unchanged. Moreover, Luke recognizes the enslaving influence of wealth and status. Again and again in the Gospel the desire for wealth and status is seen as the main threat to true discipleship (6:20, 24; 8:14; 12:15–34; 14:33; 16:9). "No servant can serve two masters. Either he will hate the one and love the other, or he will be devoted to the one and despise the other. You cannot serve both God and Money" (16:13–14).

A church in a prosperous town with twenty-seven thousand inhabitants received over sixty applications for the post of assistant pastor. At the same time a church in northern England with an established evangelical ministry serving a city of several hundred thousand people could not get one application for the post of assistant pastor. People sometimes claim it is a question of calling. They do not dispute the validity of ministry to the poor but feel their calling is to the rich. That is not Luke's pitch to Theophilus. And it does not explain why God apparently calls far more people to prosperous areas than he does to the poorer areas of the nation! In reality the only call in the Bible is the call to the way of the cross, the way of service, sacrificial love, and suffering.

In 1 Corinthians 1 Paul says:

> *Brothers, think of what you were when you were called. Not many of you were wise by human standards; not many were influential; not many were of noble birth. But God chose the foolish things of the world to shame the wise; God chose the weak things of the world to shame the strong. He chose the lowly things of this world and the despised things—and the things that are not—to nullify the things that are, so that no one may boast before him. It is because of him that you are in Christ Jesus, who has become for us wisdom from God—that is, our righteousness, holiness and redemption. Therefore, as it is written: "Let him who boasts boast in the Lord." (vv. 26–31)*

God has a strategy to exalt his Son and magnify his grace. That strategy is to choose the foolish, weak, and lowly people of the world as his own. The world esteems the intellect of professionals, the influence of the powerful, and the nobility of the upper classes. It thinks these things matter. But our boast is in Christ Jesus. He alone is our righteousness, holiness, and redemption. Our standing before God is wholly unrelated to our intellect, social class, or wealth. It is all of his grace. And so there can be no mistake or confusion, God chooses the lowly, the poor, the unrespectable, and the marginalized to populate his kingdom. He does this to shame and nullify human pride. This is great! Those the world esteems are nothing in the kingdom of God. And those the world despises, God exalts. He lifts them up and gives them places of honor. And unless we adopt their despised and lowly status, we can have no part in God's topsy-turvy kingdom (Matthew 18:1–5). God gives the gift of faith disproportionately to the marginalized.

This is reality. The church today is growing among the shanty towns of Africa and the *favelas* and *barrios* of Latin America. When we look at the church throughout the world, God is choosing the weak and lowly to shame the power and wealth of the West. It seems that God's response to the imperialism of global capitalism is to raise up a mighty church in the very places this new empire marginalizes and exploits. Let the Western church take note.

The big question is, why is the church in the West failing to reach the poor and marginalized in our society? If our churches do not reflect the reality Paul describes in 1 Corinthians 1, then we have to ask ourselves, concerning the message we have proclaimed, the way we have proclaimed it, the church cultures we have created, the expectation we have of church members, whether in some or all of these ways we have been untrue to the message of the cross. We have left room for boasting. Instead of nullifying status, intellect, and wealth, we have valued these things too highly and so nullified the message of "Jesus Christ and him crucified" (1 Corinthians 2:2). Conservative Christians are right to oppose any downgrade in the doctrine of substitutionary atonement.[6] But we must examine ourselves to see whether we too are robbing the cross of its power.

5

CHURCH PLANTING

TO ASK HOW THE PRINCIPLES OF GOSPEL, mission, and community apply to church planting is to ask the wrong question. Mission and community do not *apply*. Church planting is the out-working of mission and community. It is the point where mission and community intersect. It is by definition a missionary activity, arguably *the* missionary activity or the core missionary activity. It ensures mission is at the heart of church life. But church planting is by definition a church activity. It ensures that church is integral to mission activity. It defines mission activity as forming and building churches. Church planting puts mission at the heart of church and church at the heart of mission.

MISSION AT THE HEART OF THE CHRISTIAN COMMUNITY

A friend of mine became a Christian in his twenties. He was a merchant seaman and had never been to church until he was converted. He tells how he was so excited about his first church business meeting. He had been to a few Sunday meetings and had been baptized. Now his first quarterly church meeting was coming up, and he was really looking forward to it. This, as he puts it, was where they were going to plot the downfall of Satan. He was in for a big shock. He discovered the main issue for discussion was the type of toilet paper they should have in the restrooms. It was a big disappointment!

Emil Brunner famously said, "The church exists by mission as a fire exists by burning." It is sometimes said that worship, rather than mission, is the central purpose of the church. But this is a false dichotomy. It is true that the church has been brought into being to give worship to God. It exists to be the bride of Christ. But Jesus does not take us up to join the heavenly choir at our conversion. Jesus left his church on earth, he tells us, to be his witnesses to the ends of the earth (Acts 1:8). Indeed, within history it is through mission that we declare God's praises (1 Peter 2:9). We who have drunk from the wells of salvation sing with joy. But we sing God's praises to the nations. We make God's salvation "known to all the world" (Isaiah 12:5). Within history, worship is mission, and mission is worship. Within history, the church glorifies God by making him known to the world. Within history, mission must be central to every local church.

But mission very easily becomes one activity among others in church life. It sits on the agenda alongside a list of other items, vying for attention. Or it is left to the enthusiasts to get on with it at the edge of church life. For some churches mission seems a distant dream as they struggle to keep the institution of church afloat. Putting on a weekly service is challenge enough.

Over time churches seem to acquire committees, meetings, programs, and traditions, none of which may be wrong in themselves, but which cumulatively move the church from mission to maintenance mode. Time and energy are spent making the institutions function. The energy of many churches is thus absorbed in maintaining the legacy of a program of activities and church buildings. Roles exist that have to be filled. The life of the church is geared around maintaining its structures and programs. We need to shift into "mission mode." People are beginning to say we need "missionary theology" rather than a "theology of mission." Mission can no longer be looked at as one branch of theology. All theology must be missionary in its orientation. We need the same reorientation as churches. We are in a missionary situation, and all that we do must be missionary.

Church planting is the best way for this to happen, as it inevitably and naturally shifts the church into missionary mode. Mission once again defines the nature, purpose, and activity of the church. This is true for both the church plant and the sending church. Indeed the sending church commonly sees more immediate growth. The church plant takes time to find its identity and build links in its community. The sending church finds people stepping up to the plate, filling the gaps left by those who have been sent. It has more relational and physical space for new people. Most important of all, its congregation is confronted afresh with the challenge of mission.

CHRISTIAN COMMUNITY AT THE HEART OF MISSION

At the heart of God's plan of salvation are a family and a nation. God's purposes are not focused on many unrelated individuals but upon his people. Christ died for the elect, his bride, the church. The Bible is the story of God creating a new humanity, a new people who will be his people. "I will be your God, and you will be my people" is a central refrain running through the Bible. The church is not simply a historic convenience, a useful way of organizing discipleship and mission. No, the bride of Christ, complete and perfect, is right at the heart of the climax of salvation. And God's purposes are not only to redeem a people for himself but also to reconcile them with one another. The fall of humanity led to alienation not only from God but also from others. But in Christ the two have been made one; the dividing wall of hostility has been broken down (Ephesians 2:11–22). That is why Christian unity is so precious. God's great plan of reconciliation is now realized in the church.

If individuals were at the heart of God's purposes, then it would be quite natural to put the individual at the heart of mission, and many people do just that. But at the heart of God's plan of salvation are a family and a nation. And so the church should be at the heart of mission.

To be a Christian is, by definition, to be part of the community of God's people. To be united with Christ is to be part of his body.

The assumption of the New Testament is that this always finds expression in commitment to a local church. The centrality of the church means the centrality of the congregation or it means nothing. Commitment to the church is easy while the church is an abstract, universal reality. But the New Testament assumes commitment to real people in real local churches with all their faults and foibles.

Some people take a fluid view of church in the name of the universal church. They go to a conference, join a short-term team, participate in a parachurch organization, claiming that all these constitute their commitment to the church. There may be some validity in calling these things church in some sense.[1] But they are not a substitute for the community that the New Testament presupposes is the context of the Christian life. It is easy to love the church in the abstract or to love people short-term. But we are called to love people as we share our lives with them. This is the pathway to Christian growth and holiness. Commitment to the people of God is expressed through commitment to specific congregations.

While it may be important to talk about the universal church, the experience of church is always rooted in local Christian community. Therefore, if church is central to the purposes of God, the local congregation must be central to the practice of mission. There cannot be mission apart from the local church. The local church is the agent of mission. It is the context in which people are discipled. There can be no sustainable Christian mission without sustainable local Christian communities. The life of the Christian community is part of the gospel message of reconciliation and part of the way by which that message is communicated.

So mission cannot be done by a lone ranger. Mission must be done by a community of believers. It cannot be done in hit-and-run raids. There must be a community that can be observed and one that offers a place of belonging. When we think "mission" we must think "church." And the best way to link church and mission is through church planting.

Wrestling with the future of the faith in the profoundly secular context of Western Europe, the late Lesslie Newbigin argued that we need to reaffirm the centrality of the congregation in mission. It is neither possible nor desirable, he argues, to return to some form of Christendom. We must turn from the kind of power exercised by "the kings of the Gentiles" and accept the role of servanthood (Luke 22:25–26). But neither should we relegate winning souls to a discipleship concerned only with the private and domestic aspects of life. That would be to forsake the universal claim of the kingdom of God. Newbigin looks to the pattern of Jesus who exercised the sovereignty of God's kingdom through servanthood. How is it possible for the church truly to represent the reign of God in the world the way Jesus did? The answer, he believes, lies in the local congregation.

> I have come to feel that the primary reality of which we have to take account in seeking for a Christian impact on public life is the Christian congregation. How is it possible that the gospel should be credible, that people should come to believe that the power which has the last word in human affairs is represented by a man hanging on a cross? I am suggesting that the only answer, the only hermeneutic of the gospel, is a congregation of men and women who believe it and live by it. I am, of course, not denying the importance of the many activities by which we seek to challenge public life with the gospel—evangelistic campaigns, distribution of Bibles and Christian literature, conferences, and even books such as this one. But I am saying that these are all secondary, and that they have power to accomplish their purpose only as they are rooted in and lead back to a believing community.[2]

Newbigin argues that in the local congregation Christians find "the framework of understanding" that enables them to make sense of the world from a gospel perspective. The "plausibility structure" of the Christian community enables believers to resist the pervasive false "normality" of modernity. The gracious, gospel character of public activity is safeguarded from the tone of moral crusade through the congregation, for the congregation gratefully remembers God's grace to us in Christ. The future of the gospel in our society does not lie in adopting particular evangelistic techniques, creating Christian political parties, or pursuing propaganda campaigns, argues Newbigin. "It will only be by movements that begin with the local congregation in which the reality of the new creation is present, known and experienced, and from which men and women will go into every sector of public life to claim it for Christ, to unmask the illusions which have remained hidden and to expose all areas of public life to the illumination of the gospel."[3]

Missions consultant Stuart Murray warns against a focus on church planting that excludes other important dimensions of mission, such as working for peace and justice in society, concern for the environment, and cultural engagement.[4] But church planting must be a priority, at the very least where no church exists. This is the natural conclusion of the centrality of the church in the purposes of God. Moreover, the church provides the best context in which to ensure that all the dimensions of Christian ministry and mission are integrated. The church has often had a presence in a local community for years. That means that it is well placed to work with the poor, but also that its work is likely to be sustainable in the long term. As a Kenyan development worker based in the UK told me, "I know that when I go back to Kenya, my church will still be there, but I don't know whether my development organization will be. They are in today and could be out tomorrow, but the local church is there for years." The local church is not just working with the poor—it is the poor. Development projects may lead to sustainable development without a local church, but they cannot sustain development that is Christian without a local community of believers. The question is not a choice between planting churches and social involvement. The question is what sort of churches are planted. Are they churches with a concern for the poor that welcome the marginalized?

THE APOSTOLIC APPROACH TO MISSION

Within New Testament practice there are two models of church planting. One arises from the New Testament approach to mission, the other from the New Testament approach to church. But the distinction should not be drawn too sharply, for what we discover is that the church is at the heart of the New Testament view of mission, and mission is at the heart of the New Testament view of church. Peter Wagner identifies twelve different models of contemporary church planting.[5] Martin Robinson and David Spriggs list ten.[6] But they all divide their lists into two categories: those in which church planting takes place apart from an existing local congregation and those in which one congregation gives birth to another. This categorization broadly equates to the two models found in the New Testament.

The first is the model adopted by Paul in which a team plants a church where no churches previously existed. For Paul mission meant planting churches. In the New Testament, wherever the gospel was preached, local churches were established. In Acts, Luke deliberately portrays Paul as a church planter. This methodology involves a church planting team or an apostolic band. The team functions as a church even as a church grows up around it, providing a context for discipleship and a demonstration of Christian community.

There is a case for calling such church planters "apostles" in some sense. In Acts 14:14, for example, Barnabas is described as an "apostle" even though he was not among the foundational apostles (Ephesians 2:20). In 1 Corinthians 9 Paul defines his apostleship both in terms of his vision of the risen Christ and his work as a church planter. The term *apostle* may carry too much contemporary baggage to be recovered. What is clear is that apostolic mission was church planting.

THE APOSTOLIC APPROACH TO COMMUNITY

The apostolic churches were reproducing churches.[7] The apostolic churches met in homes—probably the homes of wealthy church members or more humble apartment blocks.[8] Not until the middle of the second century were homes specially adapted for Christian gatherings. Only later still were Christian buildings purposely built—largely to replicate pagan temples after Constantine made Christianity the civil religion of the Roman Empire.[9]

This meant they grew by adding further household gatherings rather than by adding numbers to one mega-congregation. So, for example, Paul writes "to the church of God in Corinth" (1 Corinthians 1:2) but can also talk about information from "some from Chloe's household" and how he baptized the members of "the household of Stephanas . . . the first converts in Achaia" (1 Corinthians 1:11, 16; 16:15).[10]

The apostolic churches were reproducing household churches because that is how they were established. The household was central to the model of the apostolic church planting team. In Acts 16 Lydia and the jailer's "households" are baptized, and a church is planted in Philippi. In Acts 18 the "household" of Crispus believes, and a church is planted in Corinth. In contrast in Acts 17 "a few" in Athens believe (v. 34), but we are not told of a household that believes. Could this be why it appears that no church was planted? Paul notes in 1 Corinthians 1:16 that he baptized the members of the household of Stephanas. So in his time in Corinth Paul presumably oversaw the establishment of a number of household churches within the city. The point is that he chose to establish a number of smaller churches rather than create one large congregation. In Ephesus Paul used the hall of Tyrannus but only for public discussions. Meanwhile he taught the believers "from house to house" (Acts 20:20).

Today in Central Asia, missionaries aim to see a household converted so they can form the basis of a new indigenous church. In one Central Asian town a number of individuals had been saved. The missionaries particularly asked for prayer that the husband of one of the believers, who is showing interest in the gospel, might be saved. Their prayer was not only for this, but that as a result a church might be established. That strategy appears to reflect the practice of the apostle Paul.

Paul planted household churches that would continue his mission by being missionary churches. Church planting was built into their nature. Paul planted churches as a bridge into a city. The churches would reach that city by adding further household congregations.

Constantly reproducing churches was the pattern of apostolic churches, but it was a pattern that gave fullest expression to the principles of Christian community. The household model in some way defines church. The church is the "household" of God (Ephesians 2:19–22; 1 Timothy 3:15; Hebrews 3:6; 1 Peter 4:17). The ability of a potential leader to manage his household reflects his ability to care for God's church (1 Timothy 3:4–5). For New Testament Christians the idea of *church* was synonymous with household and home. The false teachers on Crete at Ephesus "must be silenced, because they are ruining whole households by teaching things they ought not to teach" (Titus 1:11; cf. 1 Timothy 5:13). And if a false teacher comes, John says, "do not take him into your house or welcome him" (2 John 10). In both Titus and 2 John the most natural reading of the text is as a reference to local household churches.

Our point is not a slavish adherence to homes as the location for church gatherings or a denial of the value that purpose-built buildings can bring. The point is that as they grew, the apostolic churches became networks of small communities rather than one large group, to safeguard apostolic principles of church life. It matters little whether these small groups are called churches, home groups, or cells, as long as they are the focus for the life and mission of the church.

Small communities determine a *size* in which mutual discipleship and care can realistically take place. They create a *simplicity* that militates against a maintenance mentality: there are no expensive buildings to maintain or complex programs to run. They determine a *style* that is participatory and inclusive, mirroring the discipleship model and table fellowship of Jesus himself. One of the key expressions of New Testament ecclesiology is "one another" (sometimes translated "each other"). This is often missed, perhaps unsurprisingly, by academic theology. It is simply the practical expression of the priesthood of all believers. Whatever flexibility there might be about the structure of church, these principles are binding. We are to disciple and exhort one another, to love and care for one another.

Many are unenthusiastic about church planting because of assumptions that big is better. But the household model of New Testament practice was no accident. It enabled the fullest possible expression of New Testament principles. Mutuality—teaching, exhorting, caring for one another—can flourish in the family atmosphere of a small group. The priesthood of all believers finds expression when no person's contribution gets lost in the crowd. Home is a powerful dynamic for evangelism: the grace of God is powerfully embodied around an inclusive meal table, just as it was in Jesus' own ministry.[11] Meanwhile, many of the advantages of size could be gained through the cooperative activities of a network of smaller churches or a large church with a network of small groups functioning as missionary communities. All too often home groups become inward-looking because they lack a missionary mandate. Yet home groups have great potential to be a context in which Christians can do mission together as a community.

If, as seems evident from the New Testament, churches grew by continually dividing, this has profound implications for our view of church growth. A vision for church growth must be a vision for church planting.

CHURCH PLANTING AND THE RENEWAL OF THE CHURCH

Church planting is an opportunity to re-invent church along radical biblical lines. Much of the New Testament demonstrates that this was so even within the first generation of the church. It was the experience of planting churches among the Gentiles that led to the crucial gathering in Jerusalem (Acts 15). It forced the church to recognize the radical implications of the death and resurrection of the Messiah for their understanding of salvation and the people of God.

I know of a church planted by a large evangelical congregation that brought certain assumptions into the endeavor. They created a staff team with a minister, assistant minister, student worker, pastoral workers, and an administrator. They bought a church building and a home for the minister. As a result they had an annual budget of around two hundred and fifty thousand pounds excluding start-up costs. They are doing a good work, growing and exploring new areas of ministry. But if every church shares those assumptions, then most are not going to plant. Such an approach is clearly beyond the reach of most congregations. If past experience and tradition define what it means to be church, that will constrain church planting. Or church plants may run the risk of being clones—copies of sending churches. Unless we recognize this danger, church planting may in fact reduce missionary activity as smaller churches struggle to ape the programs of larger churches.

Often the main limitation to church planting is a failure of imagination. People cannot imagine how church planting might be done or how church might be done differently. People do not want to let go of the "success" their church has become. This may be because some do not want the risk, effort, and discomfort that church planting involves. But often it has more to do with their view of church. We have a notion of what a "successful" church is, and this involves a certain level of staff, programs, and activity. Church planting feels like it will involve letting this go, moving from success to lack of success.

We must not be driven by sociology or accommodate to our culture. But we need to take into account the new missionary situation in which we find ourselves. In the UK, broadly speaking, 10 percent of the population attend church regularly on a normal Sunday; 10 percent are fringe members, attending once every couple of months; 40 percent are "dechurched," having lost contact with church within their lifetime; and 40 percent have never attended church apart from the occasional rite of passage.[12] This new missionary context requires new approaches. Church planting cannot involve an uncritical replication of existing models. Church planting should be at the forefront of new ecclesiological thinking. This is the value of the twin principles of gospel and community. They provide a framework in which we can explore new ways of doing church while guarding against cultural capitulation.

There is a lesson here from the experience of cross-cultural mission. When the gospel first enters a culture, the contrast between the gospel and that culture is usually stark. Over time, however, the church not only affects the surrounding culture but also accommodates it. The Western church, for example, has shaped the value given to honesty, respect, and generosity in Western culture, but we have also been seduced by the lie that consumer goods give meaning and identity. Through mission the church can break free from external conformity to culture and internal conformity to tradition to rediscover the vitality of the gospel. Church planting is crucial to the health of the wider church. Good church planting forces us to re-ask questions about the gospel and church, to re-invent churches that are both gospel-centered without religious tradition and relevant without worldly conformity.

There need be no second-generation churches if the church is constantly reconfiguring itself through church planting. Second-generation "Christians" are those without their own living experience of the gospel. Second-generation churches are those who have lost their gospel cutting edge. It may be that a fiftieth church anniversary is not an occasion to celebrate the faithfulness of God but to lament the stagnation of his people. Far from weakening a sending church, church planting is a vital opportunity to refocus the life of the church on the gospel. The identity of the sending church should radically change. It cannot continue as the same church or repeat the same program. It must look again for new leaders to emerge. It must ask all over again how it will reach its neighborhood with the gospel.

CONCLUSION

It is sometimes said that those committed to church planting fall into two camps. The first camp includes those whose primary concern is mission and who see church (in the form of church planting) as the most biblical or most convenient way to pursue their commitment to mission. The primary concern of the second camp is the church. They see mission (in the form of church planting) as the best way to pursue their radical vision of the church.

In 1 Corinthians 3 Paul reflects on what constitutes good church planting (and it is from this chapter that the expression *church planting* comes). The key thing is that the gospel is at the heart of church planting. The Corinthian church plants had lost sight of the gospel. They were concerned with human power and wisdom. They were dividing over secondary issues. Paul puts the gospel of Christ crucified back at the heart of church and church planting.

Those whose primary concern is with evangelism can too easily get locked into pragmatism. The literature on church planting abounds with prescriptive techniques and procedures. Detailed plans are offered on topics from forming a team to holding a public launch and beyond. Paul reminds us of *the sufficiency of the gospel* of Christ crucified. People are saved and the church built through the sovereign grace of God and the power of the gospel (1 Corinthians 2:1–5). We should be careful that what we build rests on the true foundation of the gospel of Christ (3:10–11). It is God who "makes things grow" (3:7).

Those whose primary concern is church can too easily get absorbed with the internal dynamics or structures of the church, so that getting the church community life "right" becomes the priority. Paul reminds us of *the centrality of the gospel*. Our great desire should be for gospel growth. Only gospel work will survive the fires of judgment (1 Corinthians 3:12–15).

There is a third camp—those whose primary concern is gospel-centered communities, whose priority is the gospel, and who see Christian community as the natural expression of the gospel. The New Testament pattern of church life implies a regular *trans*planting of churches. This creates a missionary dynamic in which new leaders can emerge and the church can re-invent itself. Church planting is part of normal church life. At present church planting carries a certain mystique. Church planters are portrayed as a unique kind of rugged pioneer. But we need to create a culture in which transplanting is normal. Every local church should be aiming to transplant and raise up church planters.

6

WORLD MISSION

THE CENTRALITY OF THE gospel word and the gospel community apply not only on our doorstep but to the ends of the earth. God summons us both to "proclaim [his] excellencies" and to be "a people for his own possession" (1 Peter 2:9 ESV). It is our responsibility and privilege as Christians to be engaged in world mission.

A WORD FOR THE NATIONS

The prophet Isaiah had a big vision—a vision that included all nations. It was, of course, a vision inspired by God. Isaiah realized that God had chosen Abraham and his descendants for the sake of all nations (Genesis 12:3), and God's promise shaped Isaiah's vision of the future. Isaiah longed for the day when the nations will say, "Come, let us go up to the mountain of the LORD," so they could learn God's way and enjoy his reign of peace (Isaiah 2:2–4). Worship for Isaiah was to let God's salvation "be known to all the world" (12:3–5).

Isaiah issued an invitation on God's behalf: "Turn to me and be saved, all you ends of the earth; for I am God, and there is no other" (45:22). In Isaiah's vision foreigners who commit themselves to God will be welcomed as part of his people (45:56). He calls on the ends of the earth to praise the Lord with a new song (42:10–13). The book of Isaiah concludes with the promise that "all mankind will come and bow down before me" (66:23). God will do this by sending out his people in mission to "proclaim [his] glory among the nations" (66:19).

The same big vision for the nations shaped Paul's missionary activity. He often justified his ministry among the Gentiles or nations by referring to Isaiah (Acts 28:23–28; Romans 9:27–33; 15:12; Galatians 4:27). Paul believed he was seeing in his ministry what Isaiah had promised: that God would include people from all nations, Jews and Gentiles (Romans 10:11–21). Romans begins with Paul's commitment "to call people from among all the Gentiles to the obedience that comes from faith" and ends with Paul glorifying God who has revealed the gospel "so that all nations might believe and obey him" (Romans 1:5; 16:26).

The word of the God of the nations challenges us with searching questions: Does Isaiah's vision for the nations shape our missionary endeavor as it shaped Paul's? Are we looking forward to the time when God will "gather all nations and tongues, and they will come and see [his] glory" (Isaiah 66:18)?

The classic text of world mission is, of course, Matthew 28:18–20. The crucified and risen Lord has a rendezvous with his followers on a mountain in Galilee (28:16). Matthew has already highlighted the significance of a mountain at different stages in the ministry of Jesus (4:8; 5:1; 14:23; 15:29; 17:1). It was from a mountain that Jesus created his new community through a word, paralleling the constitution of Israel when Moses received the Law on Mount Sinai (5:1). It was on a mountain that Jesus revealed his glory in the Transfiguration (17:1). Now he meets his disciples on a mountain and in his resurrected glory speaks a "final" authoritative word.

The ministry of Jesus also ends where it began, in "Galilee of the Gentiles" (4:15). The area that first experienced the devastating judgment of God through the Assyrian invasion of 722 B.C. is the area where the conquering Son begins his global ministry of blessing and life (Isaiah 9:1–2; Matthew 4:12–17). Three years earlier, light had dawned to those described as being "in the land of the shadow of death." Now that light is dispersed into the entire world. The message of Jesus was a declaration of the immanent rule of God (4:17). As those sent by the One to whom all authority has been given (28:18), the disciples are to be the means by which that rule will be extended.

In the contemporary and often confused scene, *mission* has become a non-specific and slippery term. But the words of Jesus that close Matthew's Gospel provide us with a vital compass point. They make it clear that it is Jesus and his word that are the very heart of mission. *He* is the one to whom authority has been given; *he* is the one who commands his disciples to go; *his* name is among those into which people are to be baptized; it is *his* teaching that people are to obey; *he* is the one who will be with them as they go. At the heart of world mission is Jesus and the gospel word.

The term *mission* is from a Latin word meaning "sent." Jesus sends his followers out into the world with his gospel word to make other followers who will go out into the world with his gospel word to make other followers in perpetuity. Mission begins in our own hearts as the gospel word of Christ crucified is effectively applied by the Spirit. And it does not stop until the far corners of the world. It is a constant continuum because mission is what we might call the steady state of God's people. The early church understood mission very well. Vinoth Ramachandra, the IFES Secretary for Dialogue and Social Engagement in Asia, says, "Missionary outreach, both to Jews and to pagans, was not an activity tagged on later to a faith that was basically 'about' something else; rather it flowed from the very logic of the death and resurrection of Jesus."[1]

We take seriously the suffering and injustice of this world. We weep with those who weep. The parable of the Good Samaritan is universal and indiscriminate in its scope. We respond obediently to the instruction to do good to all people. We give bread to the hungry and water to the thirsty. We raise our voices on behalf of the oppressed. We demonstrate by our lives together as Christians what it means to live under the reign of King Jesus and so invite others to live under that reign. Integral to Christ's community are people whose hearts have been changed and softened so that we reach out instinctively and sacrificially to those at the margins of society. After all, that is what Jesus did, and we follow his example. As we do so, we explain our actions by commending the Savior who has so transformed us and the means by which he worked that miracle of grace.

But it is only those who have come under the reign of King Jesus who can commend him to the world and explain the message of the cross. So the proclamation of the gospel word must be at the heart of mission. Otherwise we lose our distinctive voice, and the world misses the distinctive word of Christ crucified. At the heart of world mission is the gospel word.

The gospel word is a word for the present about the future. Hope is integral to our message. Non-Christians campaign for justice and feed the hungry, often with greater energy than Christians. But only Christians can point people to the world to come. Only Christians can show them how eloquently and relevantly the Bible describes the world we all want. People may dismiss this as "pie in the sky when you die," but this is the promise of the gospel. The very best we can do for others is turn their gaze toward eternity. This is what the gospel word and gospel communities do so uniquely.[2]

In A.D. 988 Prince Vladimir of Kiev decided upon Eastern Orthodoxy as his "religion of choice," having also explored Islam, Judaism, and Catholicism. So he marched the citizens of Kiev down to the Dnieper River where they were forcibly baptized. With this event the Russians became a "Christian" people. The alternative was to be "the prince's enemy"! This is "mission" through the sword rather than through the word. Still today some Christians want to extend Christ's kingdom through the sword. They may not advocate forcible baptisms. But they expect the state to defend the interests of the church or legislate Christian values or protect the Christian heritage of their nation. So-called evangelical groups campaign to defend Christian influence in state education or a distinctly Christian coronation or inauguration oath. The cause of Christ, it is assumed, should be pursued through political means. This is the reflex of Christendom, the alliance of Christianity with earthly power. But as the Great Commission makes clear, Christ's kingdom is extended through the proclamation of the gospel. Christ's people should expect to be persecuted by the world (Matthew 5:11–12). Our King does not reign from a throne but from a cross.

A COMMUNITY FOR THE NATIONS

Psalm 67 reshapes Aaron's prayer of blessing over the people of Israel in Numbers 6:22–27. The Psalms connect the worshipper and God. Psalm 67 makes a further connection—between the worshippers, God, and the nations. The original context of the prayer is one of instructions to Moses concerning "the internal or moral and spiritual organization of the nation as a congregation of the Lord."[3] The prayer assumes Israel's distinctive identity in the world. They are the people the Lord will bless and keep, the people on whom his face will shine and to whom he will be gracious. The psalmist takes this prayer and gives it a universal focus. He calls on God to be gracious to the nation and bless them, causing his face to shine on them, so "that your ways may be known on earth" (v. 2). The remainder of the psalm calls the nations to praise Yahweh and rejoice because of him. The intent of God's blessing is summarized at the end of the psalm: "God will bless us, and all the ends of the earth will fear him" (v. 7). The psalmist knew the purpose of Israel's election and understood the determination of Yahweh to fulfill the promise he made to Abraham. He would bless the descendants of Abraham so that through them he might bless the nations and so be recognized as the God of the whole earth.

The church is God's mission strategy. At the heart of God's plan to bless the nations are the people of God. The church is formed *by* mission and *for* mission. By the word she proclaims and the corporate life she lives, men and women throughout the world are commanded to repent and invited to live. The gospel word and the gospel community are both indispensable to mission because that has always been God's strategy.

The New Testament speaks of church in two senses. First, the church is the heavenly congregation continually gathered around God's throne. Second, it is local congregations showing the reality of that heavenly church. We each have a part to play in helping our local congregation model increasingly more that heavenly congregation. We do that by extending love and grace to one another and by reaching out to others with the gospel.

I have a tree in my garden. "This is the best apple tree in the world," I tell you. You can see for yourself that it is a fine tree. The shape is exquisite, the foliage is lush, and the trunk is stout. But the only sure way of proving my claim that it is the best in the world is to taste its apples. You know a good tree by the apples it produces! So it is with the gospel. We know that the arrival of the kingdom is good news because of the kind of rule the King exercised on earth. We know it continues to be good news by the communities he creates that live life to the full and model his rule. This is why we can talk of the church as God's mission strategy. And that means real, local churches!

Both local and global mission is the privilege and responsibility of any and every local church. Christ's wisdom is "fleshed out" as his body serves the gospel together across the divides of race, culture, and language (Ephesians 3:8–11). How on earth, quite literally, do we connect this big vision with our actual experience of church? The church we see now seems full of wrinkles and blemishes, but her identity is as a beautiful bride adorned for her husband (Ephesians 5:26–27). We need that vision to shape our perspective. We need to see the church as something beautiful, dynamic, and capable of reaching the nations with the gospel word. That is how God sees her, and that is his purpose for her.

This view reflects the evidence of Paul's mission activity. In Romans 15:19 Paul says, "From Jerusalem all the way around to

Illyricum, I have fully proclaimed the gospel of Christ." The verb translated "fully proclaimed" means to bring something to completion or to finish something already begun. It is a bold and ambitious claim. The New Testament scholar Leon Morris comments, "Since Paul had done no more than preach in a number of the larger cities, this can scarcely mean that he felt that the whole of the area named had been evangelized. . . . He had preached in strategic centers throughout the area named and established churches."[4] Paul had done what was required of him. The ongoing work of reaching out from those centers to the outlying regions was the responsibility of the churches he left behind. Paul's confidence in those churches to do this is implicit in his claim. Mission was part of their DNA because the word that had given them life was God's word for the world.

The Mission of the Church and the Mission of God

Not everyone sees it this way. It has become common to draw a contrast between the *missio Dei* (God's mission) and the *missio ecclesiae* (the church's mission). David Bosch, the South African missiologist, for example, claims that when it focused on church planting as a primary means of mission, the church "ceased to point to God or to the future; instead, it was pointing to itself."[5]

Karl Barth was one of the first theologians to speak of the *missio Dei*. The term *mission*, he pointed out, was originally used of the sending of the Son by the Father and the sending of the Spirit by the Father and the Son. To this was added a further sending—the sending of the church by the Trinity. The Triune God is a missionary God. The church, then, has a mission because God has a mission. The role of the church is to participate in the mission of God. The value of this perspective is the way it roots mission in the doctrine of God rather than relegating it to applied theology. It also debunks mission as institution or empire building.

But as the twentieth century progressed, the concept of the *missio Dei* was modified in some circles. It came to be seen as encompassing all that God was doing in the world. It took place through the events of history rather than the activity of the church. The mission of the church was to be involved in the wider activity of God in the world.

The problem is that too often divine activity in history was discerned through a framework of Enlightenment values rather than through the testimony of the Bible. As a result, all sorts of activities are justified because they are part of the *missio Dei*. The *missio Dei* is often used, not to provide a wider context for the mission of the church, but as a contrast to the mission of the church.

The mission of God must be defined in biblical terms. And in the Bible, God tells us that the focus of his mission in the world is the formation of a people who will be for his own possession (Exodus 19:5). The church is not a human invention or institution but reflects and expresses the triune character and saving purposes of God. To say we should point to God and not to his church is a false distinction if God's purpose is to save a people for himself. That was the promise to Abraham, and the fulfillment of that promise forms the unifying theme of the biblical narrative.

The Mission of the Church and the Mission Agency

Imagine a jigsaw puzzle showing a cityscape. Each piece is vital, but no piece on its own can give anything like the full picture. As you build up some clusters of pieces to make, say, a few streets, you start to get a better feel of the whole. Ultimately as those clusters are joined together, you get the full picture. So it is with the church and mission. God's wisdom is displayed through the church. Each Christian is integral, but each church reveals far more of God's glory than one Christian ever could. And churches connected together show that God's wisdom is far greater and richer than one church's little corner of the kingdom could ever reveal. Understood in this way, mission is a communal project in which a number of gospel communities are involved together as they seek to extend the reign of Jesus through planting more churches.

To some this seems like crass idealism. This attitude is summed up in the words of one mission executive who said, "The problem with churches doing mission is that it doesn't work." The argument often goes that expertise and experience are in short supply in local churches, and so mission needs to be done by the professionals—big organizations with big resources and big staff teams can do big things for God. As a result, world mission is contracted out by local churches to agencies and professionals.

There may be some truth in this. But where does that leave the rest of God's people? Does the progress of the gospel in our world point to mission agencies as the total answer? Many people feared for the church in China when missionaries were expelled in 1945, but in fact church growth boomed. House churches are now sending people as missionaries to cities in China and beyond. Mission agencies are active again in China, but local churches are central to what God is doing.

In 1700 Nicolas Ludwig von Zinzendorf was born into a noble family in Dresden, in what is now eastern Germany. He studied law at university and was part of the court at Dresden. But a turning point in his life came when he met a carpenter called Christian David, who persuaded Zinzendorf to use his estate as a place of refuge for a group of persecuted Christians from Moravia (part of present-day Czech Republic). The refugees formed a new village, Hernhut, on the estate. Within five years, however, the growing community was bitterly divided, and Zinzendorf took over the leadership in 1727.

Shortly after the intervention of Count Zinzendorf, the community experienced a time of remarkable spiritual renewal, and the warring factions were reconciled. Hernhut grew rapidly and became a major influence for Christian renewal during the eighteenth century. One of the immediate consequences of this revival was the establishment of a continuous prayer watch that continued for one hundred years. This in turn shaped one of the most striking features of the Moravians, namely their radical and costly commitment to taking the good news of Christ to the far corners of the world. On one occasion Zinzendorf visited Copenhagen to attend the coronation of Christian IV. It was there that he met people from remote lands such as the West Indies and Greenland. As he heard about conditions in these places, he found himself gripped by an intense passion to reach them with the word of God.

In 1732 the Moravian community sent a team to the West Indies, and in 1733 another party headed for Greenland. Over the years the Moravians sent hundreds of missionaries to various parts of the world, including North and South America, the Arctic, Africa, and the Far East. Theirs was the first large-scale missionary movement. It was a movement distinguished by the "ordinariness" of the people sent out. The first missionaries were a potter named Leonard Dober and a carpenter named David Nitschmann who went to the Caribbean island of St. Thomas.

The apostle Paul assumed that local churches would take a common interest in mission, providing funds, coworkers, hospitality, and prayer to support the common vision (Acts 15:39–16:5; 20:1–6; 2 Corinthians 8:1–6; Ephesians 6:19–22). He organized the Jerusalem collection as a sign of the reconciliation of Jew and Gentile in one church under Christ. Individual churches can demonstrate the reconciliation of God across some divides. But how much greater the reconciling message of the gospel when churches work together in common missionary endeavor. When multinational teams work together in a similar way to the Pauline apostolic teams, they are, as it were, mobile churches. Their various cultural strengths more fully illustrate the nature of God and the multi-colored collage produced by his grace.

One example of this is a church planting team being formed to reach the six hundred thousand Albanians in Macedonia, an almost totally unevangelized group of people with perhaps just twenty Christians among them. An Albanian church is taking a leading role, providing workers and cultural understanding. A British church is providing training and workers. An American church is getting involved in leadership development. All will contribute prayer and money. These churches are not "experts" in world mission. They are simply but effectively working together as an extended gospel community to get the gospel word out to create new gospel communities for God's glory.

A Baptist church in Russia and an Anglican church in the UK are teaming up with local Christians to pioneer church planting in Mongolia. The Russian and UK churches are providing training as well as funding development projects and yurts (traditional tents) for Mongolian missionaries. The initiative is capturing the imagination of ordinary Christians. One retired Russian Christian, for example, has taken a job as a janitor simply to raise money for the project.

Another example is a relatively young church that supported pioneer church planting in Italy through financial donations and regular prayer. When its mission partner faced persecution, it sent one of its members in a show of solidarity. It was an ordinary church comprised of ordinary people—a businesswoman, a prison guard, an ex-fortune-teller. That church was the church in Philippi. Its mission partner was the apostle Paul. Paul urged them to "conduct yourselves in a manner worthy of the gospel of Christ" (Philippians 1:27). Markus Bockmuehl suggests this could be translated as "live as worthy citizens of the gospel," since this reading "takes seriously the reference to citizenship which the verb originally carries in the Greek."[6] They are not to think of themselves, first and foremost, as citizens of the Empire. They are "citizens of the gospel." They are to ask themselves: How do citizens of the gospel live? How can our ordinary lives and mundane decisions express the gospel? The net result will be a gospel identity and lifestyle in which they are "contending as one man for the faith of the gospel" (1:27).

At present the military and economic might of Western nations is struggling to counter the threat of international terrorism. It is proving difficult to defeat an enemy made up of local cells working toward a common vision with high autonomy but shared values.

They are flexible, responsive, opportunistic, influential, and effective. Together they seem to have an impact on our world far beyond what they would if they formed themselves into a structured, identifiable organization. Churches can and should adopt the same model with a greater impact as we "wage peace" on the world.

DISCIPLESHIP AND TRAINING

JESUS' FIRST ACT AT THE beginning of his ministry was to declare the imminent arrival of God's kingdom (Mark 1:14–15). His second act was to call people to follow him (Mark 1:16–20). The first act concerned the arrival of a whole new order rather than a modification of present arrangements. The second act demonstrated the reality of this. By inviting four fishermen to follow him, Jesus was actively inaugurating this new age as he formed a new community. Discipleship was common among rabbis of the day. But whereas pupils tended to attach themselves to rabbis, Jesus took the initiative by issuing a command. This was Jesus the King summoning followers. Every Christian is a disciple of Jesus because in the kingdom of God it is only Jesus who has disciples. It is legitimate to talk about Christians discipling one another as long as we recognize that we are describing the process by which disciples of King Jesus help one another to be better disciples of King Jesus.

In the chapter on evangelism we argued that both the gospel word and the gospel community are central to the evangelistic process. It is the same for discipleship. The means by which sinners are evangelized, the gospel word and the gospel community, are the means by which sinners are discipled. We continue to "evangelize" one another as Christians because it continues to be the gospel message with which we exhort and encourage one another. The good news that gives life is the good news that transforms, while the community that incarnates gospel truth for the sinner is the community that incarnates gospel truth for the saint.

Indeed Jesus defines mission as a process of discipleship. In the Great Commission he establishes the necessity and means of universal discipleship: "All authority in heaven and on earth has been given to me. Therefore go and make disciples of all nations, baptizing them in the name of the Father and of the Son and of the Holy Spirit, and teaching them to obey everything I have commanded you" (Matthew 28:18–20). The means by which the nations are discipled are baptism and teaching.

BAPTIZING PEOPLE INTO THE GOSPEL COMMUNITY

Baptism is an act of initiation, a way in. It is a dramatic act that tells a story. It speaks about dying to an old way of life, an old set of values, an old community, and a former identity. It also speaks about rising to a new way of life, a new set of values, a dynamic new community, and a revolutionary identity. Baptism is a communal act, not a solitary affair. It is how we experience the corporate, shared life of the Trinity—Father, Son, and Holy Spirit. We become disciples by becoming part of the people of God. Baptism marks our birth into the family of God. This is the context where I am *made* a disciple. The implications of the Great Commission become apparent when we see how the first disciples worked out that Commission in the book of Acts. What we discover is that it meant church planting. As the disciples went in response to the command to be witnesses to Jesus, they planted churches in Antioch (11:26), Derbe, Lystra, Iconium (14:1–26), Philippi (16:11–40), Thessalonica (17:1–9), Corinth (18:1–11), and Ephesus (19:1–10).

It is in the family of God that I am able to care and be cared for, love and be loved, forgive and be forgiven, rebuke and be rebuked, encourage and be encouraged—all of which are essential to the task of being a disciple of the risen Lord Jesus. Too often, however, churches are not contexts for making disciples so much as occasions for acknowledging relative strangers. Experience teaches that there is also an inverse ratio at work: the larger the group, the more inevitable is the superficiality of our relationships. Instead of churches growing beyond the point of being able to sustain meaningful life-on-life family relationships, an alternative (and maybe essential) strategy would be to begin new congregations through church planting.

G. K. Chesterton said, "The man who lives in a small community lives in a much larger world. . . . The reason is obvious. In a large community we can choose our companions. In a small community our companions are chosen for us."[1] Community has been insightfully defined as the place where the person you least want to live with always lives![2] Responding to this, Philip Yancey says, "We often surround ourselves with the people we most want to live with, thus forming a club or clique, not a community. Anyone can form a club; it takes grace, shared vision, and hard work to form a community."[3] We might also add that it takes a miracle that only God himself can perform. But it is in such a community that disciples are made. To be a community of light from which the light of Christ will emanate we need to be intentional in our relationships—to love the unlovely, forgive the unforgivable, embrace the repulsive, include the awkward, accept the weird. It is in contexts such as these that sinners are transformed into disciples who obey everything King Jesus has commanded.

TEACHING PEOPLE THE GOSPEL WORD

Babies are not just born into families and then left there. In functioning families, they are nurtured and prepared for adulthood. For all the talk of peer pressure and the influence of the media, the primary influence on a child is the family. This is the context in which children learn values. But not much of that teaching occurs in formal "sit down and listen to Mother or Father for forty-five minutes" contexts! Most of it is done in life settings as situations crop up. Most of it happens in conversations as you are out walking the dog or washing the car. Much of it is in response to events in which someone has messed up, misbehaved, or made an error of judgment—all actions that in some way reveal what is going on in our hearts.

All too often people equate being word-centered with being sermon-centered. People argue for sermons by arguing for the centrality of God's word, assuming that the word and the sermon are synonymous in Christian practice. It assumes God's word can only be taught through sermons. Or people assume that the alternative to sermons is anarchy or relativism with no place for the Spirit-gifted teacher of God's word, as if Spirit-gifted teachers can only exercise their gift through forty-five-minute monologues.

But our concern is not to reject the sermon. Monologue continues to have its place as one of the ways in which the Bible can and should be taught. It stands alongside other complementary methods such as dialogue and discussion. Being word-centered is not less than being sermon-centered. Our contention is that being word-centered is so much more than being sermon-centered.

The reality is that there is little New Testament evidence for the sermon as we understand it today. Jesus taught primarily through dialogue, sayings, and stories. He occasionally taught in synagogues, but more often he taught in homes, along the road, and in the open air. The so-called "Sermon on the Mount" is probably a summary of a whole day of teaching, giving us little clue about the nature of interaction that went on. The sermons in Acts are for the most part unprepared defense speeches. They are not delivered from a pulpit on a Sunday morning but before a court or before a mob. When Paul does address Christians on a Sunday (and Eutychus falls asleep!), the word used to describe his teaching is the Greek word from which we get our English word *dialogue* (Acts 20:7). The word commonly translated "preach" means to proclaim the gospel to unbelievers. It covers any verbal communication including discussion, dialogue, or debate. It actually conveys what we mean when we speak today of evangelism rather than simply a forty-five-minute monologue delivered from a pulpit. Historically the sermon as monologue arose after the "conversion" of Constantine, and imperial backing for Christianity brought large numbers of nominal Christians into the church. As a result, it was no longer possible for a group of genuine followers of Christ to discuss God's word with a Bible teacher.

It should be no surprise that Jesus taught through dialogue and questions. Studies by IBM and the UK Post Office show that people who learn by hearing alone retain just 10 percent of what they have learned after three months. People who learn by hearing, being shown, and experience retain 65 percent. This means the only person experiencing good learning in a sermon is the preacher!

> Adults have experience and can help each other learn. Encourage the sharing of that experience and your sessions will become more effective . . . so adults need to relate learning to their experience. . . . Adults learn best in an atmosphere of active involvement and participation . . . so adults need the opportunity to participate. . . . Adults learn best when it is clear that the context of the training is close to their own task or jobs. Adults are best taught with a real-world approach . . . so learning needs to be related to real issues.[4]

Word ministry takes place in a variety of ways, not simply for forty-five minutes on a Sunday morning. It takes place through group Bible studies. It takes place when two people meet to read the Bible. It takes place as people are mentored through the word. In our experience, most character formation and discipleship takes place through informal and ad hoc conversations. This kind of word ministry requires relationships, time, and gospel intentionality.

But being word-centered is more than how you teach and disciple people. It means governing church life by God's word. It means every decision, formal and informal, is explored through explicit reference to God's word. We ask, and re-ask, what God's word teaches about the issues and problems we face.

James says, "Do not merely listen to the word, and so deceive yourselves. Do what it says" (James 1:22). We must not only listen to the word—we must put it into practice. Churches are full of people who love listening to sermons. But sermons count for nothing in God's sight. We rate churches by whether they have good teaching or not. But James says great teaching counts for nothing. What counts is the *practice* of the word. What counts is teaching that leads to changed lives. We must never make good teaching an end in itself. Our aim must be good learning and good practice. And that is a radically different way of evaluating how word-centered we are.

Being word-centered means God's word has priority over tradition and precedent. Many churches that claim to be word-centered are in practice tradition-centered. From time to time I ask people how they have changed their views over the past few years. It is telling when people cannot think of an answer. Unless someone long ago came to a complete and perfect understanding of the Bible, it suggests people are no longer living under God's word so that it challenges their thinking and practice.

TEACHING "ALONG THE ROAD"

This life context and word content for discipleship reflects the setting of the great summary of Israelite faith: "Hear, O Israel: The LORD our God, the LORD is one. Love the LORD your God with all your heart and with all your soul and with all your strength" (Deuteronomy 6:4–5). Israel's identity as a people was tied up with the "word" spoken to them by the Lord. It was God's word that constituted them as his people at Sinai (Deuteronomy 5:4; Hebrews 12:19). Peter Adam says, "The basic structure of the theology of Deuteronomy is that God has spoken. . . . The command 'Hear O Israel' is characteristic of Deuteronomy . . . followed by instructions to remember, teach, discuss, meditate on and practise the words of God."[5] This creates a "verbal spirituality" in which the only appropriate response is to "love the Lord your God with total commitment, with your total self, to total excess!"[6] What is significant for the practice of discipleship is the way the book of Deuteronomy then brings both this lofty theology and all-encompassing commitment down to earth: "These commandments that I give you today are to be upon your hearts. Impress them on your children. Talk about them when you sit at home and when you walk along the road, when you lie down and when you get up" (Deuteronomy 6:6–7). This truth and its response are for everyone, and the way to teach them is in the routine of life. Chris Wright says, "The law was to be the topic of ordinary conversation in ordinary homes in ordinary life, from breakfast to bedtime."[7]

This is not to denigrate the importance of formal teaching times at church but rather to emphasize the need also to bring teaching out of the pulpit and embed it in life. Just as the Law defined Israel's identity and shaped her life, so the word of God is to define what we are as the church. And that process of definition occurs in the mundane setting of everyday life and relationships. The gospel word should be central to a formal meeting, but it also has to be the heart of all we do as the people of God and how we relate to the world.

The teaching along the road in Deuteronomy 6 is seen in the ministry of Jesus. He taught as he met the sick, as he answered questions, as he ate with people, as he walked along the road. Chapters 9–10 of Mark's Gospel are an extended explanation of what it means to be a disciple of Jesus. And all this teaching takes place along the road. And it is not any old road. It is the road to Jerusalem. It is the way to the cross. And that mirrors the teaching. To be a disciple, as Jesus keeps reminding the twelve, is to follow the way of the cross.

We should be teaching one another the Bible as we are out walking, driving in the car, or washing the dishes. People should learn the truth of justification not only in an exposition of Romans 5 but as they see us resting on Christ's finished work instead of anxiously trying to justify ourselves. They should understand the nature of Christian hope not only as they listen to a talk on Romans 8 but as they see us groaning in response to suffering as we wait for glory. They should understand the sovereignty of God not only from a sermon series on Isaiah but as they see us respond to trials with "pure joy" (James 1:2). We have found in our context that most learning and training takes place not through programmed teaching or training courses but in unplanned conversations—talking about life, talking about ministry, talking about problems.

Let us make a bold statement: truth cannot be taught effectively outside of close relationships. The reason is that truth is not primarily formal; it is dynamic. The truth of the gospel becomes compelling as we see it transforming lives in the rub of daily, messy relationships. Jay Adams says, "A whole person will affect whole persons on all levels; that is the goal of discipleship training. . . . It all involves commitment to God. Therefore, truth incarnated in life is the goal. For reaching this goal, only one method is possible—the biblical one—discipleship. Whole persons must teach whole persons; the Word must be made flesh."[8]

You could start simply by telling someone today about your relationship with God or your struggles with sin. Tell him or her about how God has encouraged you, answered your prayer, spoken to you through the Bible, and given you opportunities to share the gospel or serve other Christians. And then ask that person about his or her walk with God. Make it a habit to talk about these things together "along the road."

TRAINING "ALONG THE ROAD"

The same principles apply to training people for leadership roles. Alongside teaching "along the road," we need training "along the road." We are not against theological colleges, but we need a big switch of focus from the isolation of residential theological colleges to apprenticeships in the context of ministry. This is how Jesus trained people. This is how Paul trained people. In residential colleges the academy sets the agenda. With on-the-job training, ministry and mission set the agenda.

Name: Ruth
Occupation: Full-time mother
Church: The Crowded House, Loughborough

In Ruth's eyes a sign that The Crowded House is taking root in Loughborough is that four couples within the congregation now own houses in the area. Not that they're chasing the "ultimate" dream of home ownership, but as Ruth observes, things are finally taking on a permanent feel. And in a town where many of the Bengali and Muslim population are unreached with the gospel and for one reason or another planning to put down roots in the area, long-term gospel ministry is vital.

Working alongside her congregational leader husband Jonny, Ruth, a mother of two preschool children, has her hands full, but she wouldn't have it any other way. "When Jonny and I moved to Loughborough, it was to help with the Student Christian Union on the local campus," she says. "Pretty soon it became clear that the level of support students needed wasn't being met by the surrounding churches." It was this that Ruth believes propelled her and Jonny to start thinking about church differently.

Ruth set out running small-group Bible studies with some of the young female students. Soon their house resembled a campus cafe with students turning up to be with the family. "We're trying to get young students to see what our lives look like, to model Christian living to them," she says. "A lot of what we do now is quite informal, but intentional."

Ruth and the wife of another leader have even formalized a small crafts business that, apart from providing income, helps them get to know students and provide them with practical skills such as cooking. And what about the strain of putting a couple of young children into the mix? "Having children hasn't really changed things that much," she concludes. "Besides, in building the kind of community we have here, we've had so much support."

For Ruth the local community is a long-term project, and her next move will be to solidify some of the local relationships with their Bengali neighbors. "Most people would look at our house and think it's a starter home," she laughs. "It's not considered a desirable place to stay, but we're here forever as far as I am concerned!"

Colleges also suit a certain type of person, and this then shapes a view of what it means to be a church leader. Most church leaders today are middle-class graduates who were trained in a college and whose qualification for ministry is a degree. The first apostles were from very mixed social backgrounds, most with no education. They trained by accompanying Jesus, and their qualification for ministry was that they knew Jesus. When the Jewish leaders "saw the courage of Peter and John and realized that they were unschooled, ordinary men, they were astonished and they took note that these men had been with Jesus" (Acts 4:13). One of the reasons we have middle-class churches that are failing to reach working-class people is that we have middle-class leaders. And we have middle-class leaders because our expectations of what constitutes leadership and our training methods are middle-class. Indeed working-class people only really get into leadership by effectively becoming middle-class.

Paul had the highest education possible (Acts 22:3). It is not bad to be highly educated. But the qualities he outlines for Christian leaders are not skills-based but character-based. The focus in 1 Timothy 3 and Titus 1 is on the character of leaders—their godliness, their maturity, their example. The only skill needed is the ability to teach—and that does not necessarily mean giving forty-five-minute sermons. It is the ability to apply God's word to the life of the church and the lives of its members.

Having caught a glimpse of the benefits of mentoring when I was much younger, I made the decision early in my ministry to provide a number of young people with the opportunity to work alongside me. The aim was to see lives changed by the gospel and people equipped for gospel ministry. Integral to the process has always been relationship. These young people not only worked for me, they worked alongside me. They witnessed firsthand both how I conducted myself in public and how I related to my family. It was a life-to-life thing—close, intimate, and demanding. But how can anyone really learn what it means to be a disciple unless he or she sees someone living out his or her discipleship? How can someone learn the need of grace without witnessing the power of grace using a flawed individual? I have to confess to being skeptical of any approach to leadership training that stops short of this level of exposure and this depth of relationship. Certainly much information can be imparted, techniques can be learned, skills acquired, but without the relational dimension, it will always fall short of true discipleship.

FROM CHURCH DISCIPLINE TO CHURCH DISCIPLESHIP

The local church is the context in which we can faithfully obey the King's commands and so demonstrate the potency of his gracious rule. In a sense, church is Eden. This is God's garden in which we find all we need for life and godliness. This is where the kingdom of God is given flesh, anticipated, and demonstrated. This is where the effects of the Fall are reversed as by grace we become lovers once more of both God and others. This is God's intended arena for our discipleship and growth.

But we all know that it does not always work that way! Our lives, individually and corporately, are all too often indistinguishable from those who are strangers to the grace of God. Jesus commanded his disciples to go and disciple the nations by teaching them to obey all that he had commanded. The reason we fail to respond to that exhortation is not that the commands of Jesus are hard to comprehend. The most significant obstacle in the interpretative process is sin! This is precisely why discipleship is essential. In becoming a Christian I am a disciple, but that is an identity, not an event. I never stop being a disciple, and I never reach the point where I no longer require daily discipleship by the gospel word in the gospel community.

I have been involved in a handful of situations where the church has deemed it necessary to discipline a church member with excommunication because of persistent refusal to turn from open sin. On each occasion the issue was blatant immorality with no repentance. Everyone agreed that the behavior was wrong. Care was taken to follow the procedure of Matthew 18, not only at the level of the letter, but also trying to be true to the spirit of the instruction. All those involved were clear that it was done with a view to the restoration of the individuals concerned. However, I have never known that process to succeed in achieving that aim. Why not? After all, church discipline is biblical, and so it is legitimate to expect it to work.

I do not pretend to have all the answers, but I suspect a significant factor was that the discipline foreseen by Jesus in Matthew 18 and by Paul in 1 Corinthians 5 was meant to be the end point of a process. Our real failure was in the process leading up to it. The culture created by the leadership was not a culture of mutual discipline and care. Anyone who has a family will know that there is more likelihood of success in dealing with acute disciplinary issues with children if as parents you have shown commitment to creating an environment of care and discipline. Church discipline needs to become a daily reality in which rebuke and exhortation are normal. Without this, any form of confrontation will itself create a sense of crisis.

We need a culture of daily and mutual discipleship. Structures and programs cannot create it. It requires the sharing of lives and gospel intentionality. We need to accept that God's lordship extends over every area of our lives. This means there is no act so mundane that it lies outside the scope of the gospel. We cannot be content with a morality of negatives (do not get drunk, do not swear). We need to take responsibility for each other's godliness—not only at the level of behavior but of attitudes and underlying idolatries. Paul encourages the Christians in Ephesus to "speak the truth in love" to one another (Ephesians 4:15.). This means recognizing that apparently insignificant moments are actually full of significance.

Grumbling, for example, is almost a national pastime and a feature of many conversations. We grumble about anything and everything. But Christians are called to stand out by not complaining (Philippians 2:14–15). So when I grumble, I need God's people gently to rebuke me and remind me of God's grace in Christ. I need them to encourage me to live a life of thankfulness so that I might "rejoice in the Lord always" (Philippians 4:4). We do this lovingly and gently, recognizing that we are all sinners saved by grace and recognizing that transformation is God's work that he will complete by that same grace.

SHEPHERDS WHO ARE SHEEP

It is important that leaders see themselves and are seen by others as part of the church. Professionalism is always the enemy of authentic gospel leadership. Leaders are not a special class set apart on their own, having to face burdensome responsibilities and forced to endure a lonely existence. Leaders cannot be detached. They must be visible believers who live their lives openly in the midst of the believing community. Jesus put it into perspective when he contrasted the leadership style of the religious leaders of his day with that of the leaders in his kingdom:

> *"But you are not to be called 'Rabbi,' for you have only one Master and you are all brothers. And do not call anyone on earth 'father,' for you have one Father, and he is in heaven. Nor are you to be called 'teacher,' for you have one Teacher, the Christ. The greatest among you will be your servant. For whoever exalts himself will be humbled, and whoever humbles himself will be exalted." (Matthew 23:8–12)*

It is both reassuring and challenging to discover that the shepherds of God's flock are first and foremost sheep! In Romans 12 leadership is a vital gift of God for the church, but one that nestles discreetly among the other gifts (v. 8).

One of the great benefits of this practice is that it abolishes, so to speak, the laity. The only demarcation among the people of God is that of function, not position. If my role is that of a leader in the local church, then I am a gospel minister using my gift to serve God's people. But whatever my role, I am still a gospel minister using my gift to serve God's people. A leader is not a "special" case: he is a servant of the gospel among gospel servants, a brother among his brothers and sisters.

This model also abolishes, so to speak, the clergy! Many of my "minister" friends speak of church as something from which they must seek solace. They protect their day off and guard the privacy of their home. They feel the loneliness of ministry, looking outside the local church for people who will pastor them and events that will refresh them. For us church is where we find solace. The Christian community pastors and refreshes me through the word of God. Someone put it to us like this: "If I were to say I needed a weekly day off from my wife and children, people would say I had a dysfunctional marriage. So why, if I say I need a day off from church, do people not ask whether I have a dysfunctional church family?"

Someone was bemoaning to me the number of congregations in their church association without "ministers." "Where are the young people coming into leadership?" they asked. As I reflected on this heartfelt question, I thought of the great young people we have working with us, sacrificially committed to gospel ministry and far more mature than I was at their age. The young people are there, but they do not want to be "the minister," expected to be omnicompetent, leading on their own.

One of the questions we get asked that makes us laugh is how many staff members we have at The Crowded House. The answer is none. But each congregation has a team of people committed to gospel ministry and church planting. Most work full-time in secular jobs. Some have chosen to work a three- or four-day week to create time for gospel relationships outside the workplace. Only two or three have funding to free them for specific ministries. In a sense all of them are staff, though none receives a salary. When we meet, the financial arrangements of people make no difference to their authority or status. It is irrelevant whether they are "full-time," "part-time," or in secular employment. Indeed, secular involvement actually enriches people's ministries, giving them a day-to-day experience of life in the world, as well as opportunities in the workplace. Dave devoted a whole year to a congregation. Initially he was disappointed when asked to get a part-time job. He did not think it would be as good as being "full-time" in ministry. But looking back he acknowledges its benefits—experience in the secular workplace, contact with unbelievers, and self-discipline. Sometimes people feel the pressure of time, but when there is a team, ministry does not fall on one or two. We also try to maintain a culture in which people are not expected to do more than is possible. We pour ourselves into Christian service but also remind one another that it is Jesus who builds his church and justifies his people.

We do not always get it right, but this is the philosophy of ministry to which we aspire. If we are going to reach the nations through planting churches, then we will need to be much more flexible and creative about the financial support of gospel work.

8

PASTORAL CARE[1]

THIS IS ONE OF THOSE "What happens next?" situations. Sarah struggled to explain the problem to Ian and Jayne. She was certain they ought to know but wasn't sure how to proceed. The silence began to feel a little awkward; so she gulped, took a deep breath, and began her story. Jayne looked at Ian with one of those concerned but caring glances. Ian suddenly realized how much he didn't know. With only a few years of pastoral ministry behind him, this seemed way out of his league.

Sarah told them she was a habitual self-harmer, and although she was in her mid-twenties, it was an established pattern. She showed them some of the scars on her arms. Jayne visibly winced at the sight of them. Where on earth should they start? What could they possibly say? If he was honest, Ian's biggest problem was comprehension: he could not even begin to understand why she would do such a thing. He felt simultaneously repulsed by and protective toward Sarah, and that ambiguity troubled him. Jayne went over and put her arm around the troubled young woman sitting in their front room, while Ian began to pray quietly.

So what happens next? Here are two possible scenarios:

#1 After the prayer, Ian tells Sarah that it would be irresponsible of him to try to deal with the problem. He was more than ready to admit that it was beyond both his knowledge and his experience.

He would gladly find the name of a psychologist and make the necessary introduction. Of course, both he and Jayne would gladly go with Sarah to the appointment, and they would definitely be there for her whenever she needed them. But it seemed wisest to get professional help.

#2 Ian is very upfront with Sarah about his reaction and the overwhelming sense of inadequacy he feels. He is convinced, however, that Sarah is in the best possible place for the issues to be worked through—not their front room, but the church! She is among people who love her, and together they can rely on the sufficiency and power of God's word. He knows it is not going to be easy. There is no magic wand to wave. But there seems to be no better place to start than with the word of God skillfully applied by the Spirit of God among the people of God.

One of the most significant issues faced by anyone involved in pastoral care is the explosion in counseling within contemporary Western society. There is something of a therapy culture developing. An increasing number of people in local churches are seeking guidance on life issues and help in handling emotional issues. Sometimes, as in Sarah's case, those emotional issues are particularly acute.

The problem with this therapy culture, according to Frank Furedi, professor of sociology at the University of Kent, is the way it has made therapy into a way of life.[2] People are encouraged to define themselves as victims who have suffered at the hands of parents, employers, or through pregnancy and any number of other things. A belief system has emerged, the credo of which is that people cannot cope "on their own." Furedi argues that a therapy culture is bad for individuals and a significant threat to public health. As long as people are encouraged to seek professional counseling to help them with everything from dealing with an unpleasant incident to raising their children, argues Furedi, individuals become disinclined to depend upon each other in the normal routine of relationships. Relationships are increasingly "professionalized."

In a brutally honest account of his life, written with his therapist, Paul Gascoigne, the former international soccer star, reveals a number of psychological conditions with which he has been "diagnosed," including obsessive-compulsive disorder (OCD).[3] Gascoigne says, "My OCD went off the scale. I'd leave the lights off in the house and I'd be going around in the dark so as not to have to worry about turning the lights off and checking them. Then I'd want a drink or a painkiller to calm me down. People don't understand why you can't stop [drinking], but there's always this voice in my head saying, 'Have another, have another.'"[4] For Gascoigne and his therapist, it seems that "the voice" is the culprit and Gascoigne is the victim. But how does such a view help someone in such obvious need? It seems that in a moment of despair, Gascoigne opened his Bible and called out to God. But the danger is that God is absorbed by an existing worldview and so becomes little more than another therapy.

This book is a call to a dual fidelity to the gospel word and the gospel community. It is our conviction that the gospel word and the gospel community do not fail us when it comes to pastoral care. Together they provide a secure framework within which to approach pastoral issues.

THE SUFFICIENT GOSPEL WORD

Is it naive or irresponsible to believe that the Bible gives not only an accurate and sufficient analysis of the human condition but also an effective response or "treatment"? Many people think so, and as a result a dichotomy is created between the ministry of Bible teaching and that of pastoral counseling. The former is considered the preserve of the "minister," while the latter is for qualified (in a secular sense) members of the wider community. Ian's response in the first scenario exemplifies this attitude and would be, by many people, considered a humble, wise, and caring response to Sarah's painful issue. But is that necessarily the case?

At the heart of historic evangelicalism is a commitment to the Bible as "the final authority on all matters of faith and conduct."

This confession has been summarized as the sufficiency of Scripture, and this is where the debate is centered.

One view argues that God has given us two books through which to understand the world—Scripture and nature. Humans, though distinctive in being made in God's image, are also part of nature. This means we can be studied and analyzed along with other animals and the rest of creation. The biblical worldview gives us a basis for scientific investigation. As a result it is possible and admirable to engage in "scientific counseling," using the services and resources of psychology and psychiatry. In fact, a failure to do so is ill-advised and irresponsible.

Another view sees the Bible as unique and altogether distinctive in the way it defines what we are as human beings. This position argues that God has revealed all we need to know about how to live lives that please and honor him. The Bible addresses the entire range of problems we experience in living in this world. Biblical truth is not limited to a narrow sphere of life, nor to a limited range of beliefs or convictions. It addresses all the basic and essential issues of what it means to be human, both in our sin and in our salvation. In 2 Peter 1:3–4 the apostle asserts:

> *His divine power has given us everything we need for life and godliness through our knowledge of him who called us by his own glory and goodness. Through these he has given us his very great and precious promises, so that through them you may participate in the divine nature and escape the corruption in the world caused by evil desires.*

Something remarkable and almost incredible has happened to Christians: we "participate in the divine nature." John Calvin comments, "The purpose of the gospel [is] to make us sooner or later like God; indeed it is, so to speak, a kind of deification."[5] Peter describes this gospel as God's "very great and precious promises." These are the means by which transformation takes place. God has called us by his own glorious goodness to know Christ. That call comes to us in the gospel, and that knowledge of Christ is ours in the gospel. There is no knowledge of Christ outside of the gospel. The Christ who saves is the Christ we meet in the Bible. Salvation is ours as the Holy Spirit takes the good news of Christ crucified and applies it to our minds and hearts in this transforming encounter with Christ in the gospel word by which we come to know God truly. And so Peter can say we have been "given . . . everything we need for life and godliness." The resources to live life well, which means living as the lovers of God and of others we were made to be, are ours in the living word of God. "Simply by being Christians, we have access to everything we need to live a life that pleases God."[6] This is the doctrine of the sufficiency of Scripture, and this is what gives us confidence in our pastoral care as we expose each other to the gospel word.

Yet there are those who would critique this perspective as reductionistic. Pastoral care in the "real" world, it is claimed, has to be far more sophisticated, nuanced, and insightful. One academic psychologist, in personal correspondence, phrased it like this: "Within the mental health world, most respected and experienced practitioners take the view that problems are always complex in their aetiology [root cause], usually as a result of an exquisite interaction between biological, psychological, social and yes, spiritual factors; but it is never the case that the aetiology is confined to only one of these domains."

The theologian and psychiatrist Richard Winter cites a complex interaction of various causes in his study of depression. One of these contributory factors is loss and separation. He points to the hymnwriter William Cowper as a case study. Cowper's mother died when he was just six. His whole sense of security rested in her presence, and when she was gone, it was as if his whole world was shattered. "He never really got over his loss, for she was like 'an omnipotent goddess' of that golden age when he was absolutely happy. . . . Cowper's grief was compounded by the lack of a close relationship with his father and by being sent off to boarding school shortly after his mother's death."[7]

What are we to make of this analysis? For a child of six years old to lose his mother is desperately sad, and to be sent away to school soon after is terribly harsh. These are clearly contributory factors. In addition, we have no way of knowing, for example, the chemistry of Cowper's brain and how helpful medicine might have been. But are these events sufficient to explain Cowper's desperate lifelong battle with depression? Was Cowper a depressive because of his circumstances or his chemistry? We do not know what was primary or secondary in his life and experience. But is it illegitimate to ask whether he, along with all of God's people, had what he needed for life and godliness through his knowledge of him who called him by his own glory and goodness? Are we to say that the gospel word had little or nothing to say to Cowper or that it has little or nothing to say to people like Sarah?

However complicated the causes of Cowper's struggles, in Christ he had the resources to respond in a godly way. If we subscribe to a view that makes our "complex aetiologies" responsible for our behavior and attitudes, then we put our lives at the mercy of our genes or our parents or our chemistry or our past. Ultimately we make those multiple factors sovereign over our lives. Of course, they can be significant factors, but we have in the precious promises of the gospel all we need to respond to those factors in a way that results in godly behavior and godly attitudes. Such a response may not be easy. It may involve a daily struggle. But it is possible.

Listen to the great eighteenth-century American theologian Jonathan Edwards as he addresses God's word to lives like Cowper's and Sarah's:

> Love to God disposes men to see his hand in everything; to own him as the governor of the world, and the director of providence; and to acknowledge his disposal in everything that takes place. And the fact that the hand of God is a great deal more concerned in all that happens to us than the treatment of men is, should lead us, in a great measure, not to think of things as from men, but to have respect to them chiefly as from God—as ordered by his love and wisdom, even when their immediate source may be the malice

or heedlessness of a fellow-man. And if we indeed consider and feel that they are from the hand of God, then we shall be disposed meekly to receive and quietly to submit to them, and to own that the greatest injuries received from men are justly and even kindly ordered of God, and so be far from any ruffle or tumult of mind on account of them.[8]

Is that not the gospel truth that Cowper needed to hear and believe? Is this not precisely the kind of truth that should be spoken gently to Sarah as she begins to come to terms with her past and her turmoil? It is certainly what I need to hear and believe.

I wish, for example, someone had spoken those truths to me a number of years ago. A good friend unexpectedly turned on me and accused me of failing him as a friend and mentor, leading him to put as much distance as possible between us. It is hard to describe how I felt. It was certainly the blackest period of my life. I could not work, my appetite was affected, my sleep pattern disturbed. There was little or no enjoyment in anything. I was hurt. I felt unjustly accused. I felt misunderstood, isolated, abandoned, and betrayed. Looking back, depression seems to be the most appropriate description of my condition.

In that darkness I needed to hear the truth of which Edwards so eloquently wrote. What glorious truth to "own that the greatest injuries received from men are justly and even kindly ordered of God"! I may not have been able to understand God's dealings with me because he is often inscrutable, but the cross assures me that he is altogether good and that his grace is magnificently sufficient.

I also needed to look at my own heart and self-righteousness. During that period of my life, I needed to see the idols that had been exposed, primarily that king of all idols—me! I felt justified both in claiming to be unable to love God and refusing to love others at that particular moment of my life. What I have come to see since is that in all of the messiness and pain of that time, I was the chief sinner who turned in on himself and so turned away from God and from others. Of course, I was to some extent a victim, but I was also a player. I was the one who committed that most heinous of sins—I had sought to be my own savior.

Were chemical factors involved? They may well have been. There were mood swings I had never known before or since. Were other factors present? It came at the end of a particularly demanding time of life in which I was emotionally drained. The day my friend broke the news to me, I had gone to a hospital for a painful eye condition associated with stress and being physically run down.

But whatever part these factors played in my situation, they were not the cause of my reaction. They were the circumstances in which my reaction took place. I had an opportunity to prove God, to find refuge in him, and to demonstrate the power of the gospel to enable me to love those who did not love me. The truth as it is in Jesus is that which could and should have equipped me to know what Paul knew:

> We are hard pressed on every side, but not crushed; perplexed, but not in despair; persecuted, but not abandoned; struck down, but not destroyed. We always carry around in our body the death of Jesus, so that the life of Jesus may also be revealed in our body. For we who are alive are always being given over to death for Jesus' sake, so that his life may be revealed in our mortal body. So then, death is at work in us, but life is at work in you. . . . Therefore we do not lose heart. Though outwardly we are wasting away, yet inwardly we are being renewed day by day. For our light and momentary troubles are achieving for us an eternal glory that far outweighs them all. So we fix our eyes not on what is seen, but on what is unseen. For what is seen is temporary, but what is unseen is eternal. (2 Corinthians 4:8–18)

What are the alternatives to this approach to pastoral care? Is our role to offer sympathy with the person suffering from cancer, depression, rejection, job loss, anorexia, moral failure, or amputation? Of course it is! Weeping with those who weep is not a pastoral technique to be learned—it is a heart response experienced as the Holy Spirit makes us more like Christ. Yet among God's people more is called for and far more is possible. All of those circumstances are consequences of living in our fallen world, and as Peter reminds us, it is in this world that we have all we need for life and godliness through our knowledge of God. Sarah will certainly have "issues" that need talking through, and her habitual self-harming should evoke a sense of profound grief from us. But Sarah needs more than Ian and Jayne's sympathy, and in the sufficient word of God they have far more to give her.

The term *spiritual* is not simply another category alongside biological, physical, environmental, upbringing, or relationships. Each of those forms of suffering, passive or active, is always and at some point a spiritual and theological issue. Part of the hope the gospel gives me is in understanding that I have a God-given responsibility together with a corresponding God-given ability to respond in a way that honors him as my all-sufficient Savior.

In Christ and the gospel word there is sanity. His "living and active" word "penetrates even to dividing soul and spirit, joints and marrow; it judges the thoughts and attitudes of the heart" (Hebrews 4:12). This penetrating word reveals our problems of behavior as essentially problems of belief. The struggles we have when our emotions seem liable to rule or define us are essentially struggles of belief in God's promises. That is why we can have confidence in the Bible to speak directly and effectively to our circumstances. Pastoral care is therefore first and foremost the ability to address the gospel word to the problems of people's lives.

THE EFFICIENT GOSPEL COMMUNITY

If our primary identity is as persons-in-community, then our ability to thrive will be shaped by our involvement in a community. Life as it should be lived is life-in-community. Community is not merely an added benefit to me. It is an essential part of what it means to be human. And this means that the Christian community is essential to what it means to be a Christian. Pastoral care in a Christian community is not merely one therapy device among many. It is the context in which any other pastoral care takes place.

The implications of this for pastoral care are highly significant. So much formal pastoral engagement takes place outside of the community, and one of the reasons for this is disengagement from the community. Sarah's sense of isolation is significant, and so Ian's determination to care for her in the context of a loving community is vital. While the need for specific counseling sessions in a more formal environment will remain, healthy engagement with others in committed relationships will deal with so many of the presenting issues and underlying causes of her problems.

Let us apply some of these convictions to the specific issue of marriage. The same difficulties faced by people outside of the church, where divorce rates are approaching 40 percent, are also those faced by people within. A significant element of this pressure is individualism. In a culture in which the rights and desires of the individual are sacred, bringing two individuals together in a relationship as close as marriage is bound to create problems. There is also a disposable attitude toward relationships in general in our society, and this affects attitudes toward marriage.

The breakup of the extended family with increased mobility has contributed significantly to the strain placed on marriage. The oft-quoted African proverb claims that "it takes a village to raise a child." But Western culture is now prepared to leave it almost entirely to a couple (and in some cases a single person). Many of the support structures of previous generations have been removed, leaving marriage exposed and vulnerable.

There is no better place for marriages to be nurtured than in a communal setting for two principal reasons.

1. *The Christian community provides the context in which we learn what it means to be persons-in-community.* This is a foundational truth if we are to live successfully with other people. If the Western world's prevailing culture reinforces individualism, a different culture is necessary to present an alternative. The church is a great context in which to learn what it means to live in relationship with others. It is the location in which my self-preoccupation will

be confronted. This happens as I hear the Bible being taught. It happens as I am encouraged and rebuked by my brothers and sisters who take responsibility for my godliness. It happens as I respond to the Lord's call to love God with all my heart and my neighbor as myself. It happens as God's truth conspires with my circumstances to show me that this is not my world and I am not God. It happens as the community responds to my sin with love and grace.

2. *The Christian community provides the best context in which marriages can flourish.* In the contemporary context, marriage is sometimes little more than "plural individualism." In the church we find practical support structures. In the church we find people who are committed to our marriage. They know from God's word what godly marriage involves and will help us live that out. They know what godly marriage involves because, whether married or single, they themselves are part of a relationship of submission and love with Christ (Ephesians 5:22–31). The church provides a wider context that prevents marriages from becoming inward-looking and self-serving.

ORDINARY LIFE WITH GOSPEL INTENTIONALITY

In the chapters on evangelism and discipleship we spoke of "ordinary life with gospel intentionality." It is the same with pastoral care. We often think of pastoral care simply as something that takes place in moments of crisis. But most pastoral care takes place in the context of ordinary life—as we eat together, wash up together, play in the park, walk along the road. This preventative care often averts pastoral crises or helps people cope when they face difficult circumstances. But for these to be occasions of pastoral care we need to be intentional about encouraging and exhorting one another with the gospel. The parallel with evangelism is no accident, for the message we speak to believers is the same as the message we speak to unbelievers—the precious promises of the gospel with the corresponding call to faith and repentance.

Often we can speak the precious promises of the gospel in ways specific to someone's needs. Here, for example, are four key life-changing truths about God:

- He is sovereign.
- He is majestic.
- He is good.
- He is gracious.

Consider someone who is anxious. They may be anxious because:

- They doubt God's sovereign control over their future.
- They fear someone's disapproval more than they fear our majestic God.
- They doubt that God's intentions toward them are good.
- In their guilt they doubt God's gracious forgiveness.

In each case they may well affirm these truths in a creedal sense. But in the pressures of the moment they lack faith in a functional sense. These examples show how pastoral issues are connected to issues of faith and truth. The passage from 2 Peter 1 above continues by describing how we should add to our faith goodness, knowledge, self-control, perseverance, godliness, brotherly kindness, and love. "But if anyone does not have them," Peter says, "he is short-sighted and blind, and has forgotten that he has been cleansed from his past sins" (v. 9). Our problem is that we forget we have been forgiven. We forget that we have all we need for life and godliness. We forget the precious promises of the gospel.

Or consider someone who is persistently worn-out. They may be worn-out:

- trying to manage their lives because they doubt God's sovereignty
- trying to win other people's approval because they fear other people more than they fear our majestic God
- pursuing material possessions because they do not look for satisfaction in our good God
- trying to prove themselves instead of trusting the justification that is ours by grace through the finished work of Christ.

Even the alternative possibilities summarized above are sufficient to warn against simplistic "solutions." Moreover, our own experience reminds us that the struggle to believe the truth is a lifelong, daily struggle. In many cases we will not understand the heart responses that underlie behavior and attitudes. But we can always speak God's word, trusting the Holy Spirit to apply it effectively to people's lives.

Marriage and self-harming are just two examples that reflect the myriad of issues faced by broken people in a fallen world. Often it is at these points of "crisis" when life is painful, difficult, and messy that the hiding places of our confidence are exposed. Ian's approach to Sarah's "problem" in the second scenario might seem bold. But it emerged from solid convictions concerning the gospel word and the gospel community. In a community where the Holy Spirit is at work through the gospel, someone like Sarah has nothing to fear. Ian was right: there is no better place to be than among the people of God when the word of God is skillfully applied by the Spirit of God!

9

SPIRITUALITY

I WAS READING A MANUSCRIPT for a publisher when a particular phrase caught my eye. It was a comment about making time for the disciplines of "contemplation, silence and solitude." It was not central to the author's argument, but it stuck in my mind. It didn't feel right. It certainly describes a good deal of what passes for spirituality among evangelicals today. Or worse than that, it constitutes a kind of advanced spirituality for the elite. We teach new Christians to pray and read their Bibles, but mature spirituality, it is said, takes us into new realms—the realms of "contemplation, silence and solitude."

But what struck me as I pondered those words is that they describe the exact opposite of biblical spirituality. Biblical spirituality is not about contemplation; it is about reading and meditating on the word of God. It is not about detached silence; it is about passionate petition. It is not about solitude; it is about participation in community. In other words, biblical spirituality reflects the dual fidelity we have argued for throughout this book. It is centered on the gospel and rooted in the context of the Christian community.

- the Bible instead of contemplation = word-centered spirituality
- petition instead of silence = mission-centered spirituality
- community instead of solitude = community-centered spirituality

SPIRITUALITY AND THE GOSPEL WORD

God reveals himself by his Spirit through his word. We do not meet God in the stillness: we meet him in his word. We are not nearer to God in a garden: we draw near to God through his word (Deuteronomy 30:14). It is Scripture breathed by the Spirit of God that is "useful for teaching, rebuking, correcting and training in righteousness." This is what makes us "thoroughly equipped for every good work" (2 Timothy 3:16–17). And it is the word of God that brings hope and change to the human heart. It is the word of God that revives our souls. The psalmist says:

> The law of the LORD is perfect,
> reviving the soul.
> The statutes of the LORD are trustworthy,
> making wise the simple.
> The precepts of the LORD are right,
> giving joy to the heart.
> The commands of the LORD are radiant,
> giving light to the eyes.
> The fear of the LORD is pure,
> enduring forever.
> The ordinances of the LORD are sure
> and altogether righteous.
> They are more precious than gold,
> than much pure gold;
> they are sweeter than honey,
> than honey from the comb.
> By them is your servant warned;
> in keeping them there is great reward.
> (Psalm 19:7–11)

Biblical spirituality is a spirituality of the word. One of the central rhythms of true spirituality is therefore reading and meditating on the Bible. Meditation is not emptying your mind, but filling your mind with God's word. There is much talk of listening to God today, and we are encouraged to hear God through stillness, contemplation, dreams, and special words. There are indeed times when God graciously guides in extraordinary ways (Acts

16:6–10), but we do not need these for godly living, and we should not make them normative. The reason is that God has already spoken. He has spoken through his Son and through his word. And he continues to speak in this way today through the Spirit. Peter says, "It was revealed to [the prophets] that they were not serving themselves but you, when they spoke of the things that have now been told you by those who have preached the gospel to you by the Holy Spirit sent from heaven" (1 Peter 1:12). The prophets spoke God's word in the past, but it is spoken to us in the present "by the Holy Spirit."

The old word is also the contemporary word. And this revelation of God is wholly adequate. It is not deficient or lacking in any way. The letter of Hebrews begins: "In the past God spoke to our forefathers through the prophets at many times and in various ways, but in these last days he has spoken to us by his Son. . . . The Son is the radiance of God's glory and the exact representation of his being, sustaining all things by his powerful word" (Hebrews 1:1–3). God once spoke in dreams and visions. But that way of communicating has been rendered unnecessary because now he has spoken by his Son. And the Son is the exact representation of God's being, and his word is powerful, sustaining all things. How can we act as if God's revelation in God's Son recorded by God's Spirit in God's word needs to be supplemented?

In the mystical and contemplative traditions, the goal of spirituality is union with Christ. Union with Christ is attained through a pattern of spiritual disciplines or a series of spiritual stages. The imagery of a ladder is often used. Gospel spirituality is the exact opposite. Union with Christ is not the goal of spirituality; it is the foundation of spirituality. It is not attained through disciplines or stages; it is given through childlike faith.

I should confess that I was once heavily drawn to the kind of spirituality represented by contemplation, silence, and solitude. I still am. But why is this? I believe it is because it represents a spirituality of achievement. It is spirituality for the elite. Biblical spirituality in contrast is a spirituality of grace. Its dominant image is that of a child petitioning its father.

It seems that a spirituality of achievement with an emphasis on spiritual insights and mysteries threatened the church in Colossae. People were claiming that while it was okay to start the Christian life through simple faith in Christ, to continue and grow you needed:

- the help of spiritual powers (2:18; see also 1:16; 2:10, 15)
- to follow regulations and disciplines (2:16–17; see also 2:11–12)
- special knowledge and "mysteries" (2:8, 18; see also 1:25–27; 2:2–4)
- to abstain from material pleasures (2:20–23)

It has become common to hear similar claims within evangelicalism. Evangelicals with their emphasis on the gospel are good at bringing people into the church, people say, but to nurture and sustain faith we need to look to other traditions—traditions offering more advanced spiritualities. We need, it is variously claimed, spiritual disciplines or mystical encounters or contemplative retreats or so-called "warfare prayer."

In response Paul emphasizes the supremacy of Christ, the fullness of revelation in Christ, and the sufficiency of Christ for Christian living. In other words, in the gospel of Christ we are richly supplied with all we need to keep going as Christians and to grow as Christians. We do not need anything else. We do not grow as Christians by moving on from Christ to more "advanced" discipleship. Instead, the message of Colossians is summed up in 2:6: ". . . just as you received Christ Jesus as Lord, continue to live in him."

SPIRITUALITY AND THE GOSPEL MISSION

Passionate Engagement

Spirituality is often used in contrast to the material. I recently had a conversation with an atheistic sociology lecturer who felt the modern world was too materialistic and needed to be more "spiritual." Christians often think in this way as well. Spirituality is seen in terms of withdrawal from the busyness of life. We have a "quiet time" or a weekend "retreat" in the country. Some people go further, believing that "spiritual" is somehow better than material. Many Christians act as if being "spiritual" is somehow set against the physical or the sexual or the bodily. But in biblical terms to be spiritual is to walk in step with the Spirit in all of life. The world God made—spiritual and material—was very good (Genesis 1:31). And the future God intends is both spiritual and material. In the bodily resurrection of Jesus, God affirms his creation and promises that one day he will purge it of evil, suffering, and ugliness and create a new heaven and a new earth. Biblical spirituality is a spirituality of the everyday in which God is glorified in all of life.

Describing humanity in rebellion against God, Paul says, "For although they knew God, they neither glorified him as God nor gave thanks to him" (Romans 1:21). Ingratitude was part of our original sin. Gratitude, in contrast, regulates our relationship with the created world by steering us between asceticism (the abstinence from earthly pleasure) and idolatry. Asceticism undervalues God's good creation, while gratitude acknowledges its value. Idolatry overvalues creation, while gratitude ensures that God remains our central focus. Hence the practice of saying "grace" at every meal, an approach we should perhaps extend to other areas (at least in terms of our attitude). If I say thank you to God for every morsel of food, that transforms that food. It is no longer merely fuel for my body; it becomes a gift from God to be enjoyed and relished. Its taste and texture take on new significance. All things are good if they are enjoyed in obedience to God's will and for his glory (1 Timothy 4:1–5).

In 1 Timothy 3:16 Paul talks about "the mystery of godliness." It is probably a catchphrase of the false teachers that Timothy must silence. Paul takes their terminology but radically recasts it: "Beyond all question, the mystery of godliness is great: He appeared in a body, was vindicated by the Spirit, was seen by angels, was preached among the nations, was believed on in the world, was taken up in glory." Jesus appeared in a body. He did the Father's work in a body, not by escaping it, and in a body he was vindicated by the Spirit. "Taken up in glory" means Christ is glorified. But how is he glorified? As he is believed on in the world. You do not find Jesus in perpetual retreat but in the world. Biblical spirituality turns out to be a spirituality of mission. We "declare the praises of [God]" by being a holy people in a hostile world, proclaiming the good news and performing good deeds (1 Peter 2:9–12).

In John 15 Jesus calls on his disciples to "remain in me" (v. 4). But this is not a passive pursuit conducted in silence. This is active faith in our union with Christ, a faith that produces fruit in the world (v. 8). We are to remain in Christ's love (v. 9). But remaining in Christ's love is synonymous with obedience to Christ's commands (v. 10). Christ does not take us out of the world but sends us into the world to "go and bear fruit" (v. 16; 17:15–18). His command is to "love each other as I have loved you" (15:12, 17). Biblical spirituality does not take place in silence; it takes place bearing a cross. It is not a spirituality of withdrawal but a spirituality of engagement. You do not practice it on retreat in a secluded house; you practice it on the streets in the midst of broken lives.

Name: Joel
Occupation: Trainee plumber and laborer
Church: The Crowded House, Sharrowvale

Joel's week is like that of many young people his age—a bit of part-time work, a bit of study or training, some soccer, and the odd night out at the pub with some mates. But there are a few telling differences. For a start, he spends time every week with several ex-prisoners with links to the church, encouraging them and helping them to get back into mainstream life. Sometimes that means just sitting and talking; at other times it means helping someone sort himself out after a drunken binge.

For Joel, life in The Crowded House is about the practical stuff. "I'm better working at the fringes," he says. "Most of my mates are from working-class backgrounds and would never set foot in a church anyway." Even the weekly soccer match is not an end in itself. As captain of the team, Joel has the respon-

Passionate Prayer

Hand in hand with passionate engagement with the world in mission is passionate engagement with God in petition.

People are often encouraged to spend time in silence and stillness before God. When most Christians I talk to try this, they end up thinking about what they watched on television the night before or compiling lists of things they need to do. As a result, they are made to feel "unspiritual." Calvin, however, says a "sweet and perfect repose" is not the characteristic of the spiritually advanced but simply of those whose "affairs are flowing to their liking." "For the saints," he continues, "the occasion that best stimulates them to call upon God is when, distressed by their own need, they are troubled by the greatest unrest, and are almost driven out of their senses, until faith opportunely comes to their relief."[1]

Biblical spirituality is not a spirituality of silence; it is a spirituality of passionate petition. If we are engaged with the world around us, we will care about that world. We will be passionate about

sibility of ensuring there is a mix of both Christians and non-Christians on the field. "We set it up for outreach," he says. "We like to keep a 60–40 split in favor of Christians, so we can influence the others in a good way."

Joel says he has two very distinct groups of friends—his Christian family at church and, in his words, "my very non-Christian mates." He believes that the greatest challenge is to hold on to this latter group because as time goes by the easy thing would be to let them go.

Unlike many of the students who come to Sheffield, Joel is fairly confident that his old mates won't be leaving the city any time soon. "They've got their lives mapped out for them already, and they're pretty much settled in Sheffield," he observes. Settling in Sheffield, as well as in the Sharrowvale congregation, is something Joel is planning to do too, and if things work out, he's planning to enter the city's police force. "I'm in it not so much for the student work but for the rest of the guys who haven't been to university who've always lived here," he says.

people's needs, our holiness, and God's glory. We will not be still in prayer. We will cry out for mercy with a holy violence. If we are silent, it will be because in our distress, words have failed us. This is the spirituality of the Psalms—a spirituality in which all our emotions are engaged. When the psalmists do talk of stilling our hearts, it is not the stillness of silence but the stilling of self-justification or self-confidence (Psalm 46; 62; 131).

In the past I have urged people in prayer meetings to spend time in praise or confession or meditation without moving on too quickly to intercession, and I have then been frustrated when they strayed into petition. But I see now that this attitude was wrong. To ask God for things is a profound act of faith. It is a recognition of his majesty, goodness, and power. It is more an act of worship than many of the songs we sing half-heartedly, for through it we acknowledge his sovereign grace. We may think of petitioning as unsophisticated. We may long for advanced techniques that smuggle some kind of achievement into spirituality. But these simple prayers truly express trust in divine majesty and truly confess our need before God. People who pray in this way are those who have really grasped the freedom of the Father-child relationship that is ours in Christ.

SPIRITUALITY AND THE GOSPEL COMMUNITY

At the heart of much evangelical piety is the individual soul before God. A personal relationship with God has all too often become an individual relationship with God. This individual relationship is seen as authentic spirituality from which other expressions of spirituality are derived. So people say things like, "We will not be prayerful in the public life of the church unless we have first learned to be prayerful in private."

In some ways it depends how you tell the Bible story. There is a version that runs something like this: "God made you to know him, but you have rejected God. Your sin cuts you off from God and brings you under his judgment. But God sent his Son to die in your place and reconcile you to God. Now you can know God and look forward to being with him after death." It is the story of an individual out of relationship with God brought back into relationship with God. This version of the story is true. But it is not the whole truth, nor is it how the Bible itself tells the story. Consider instead a different version: "God made humanity to know him and to rule over his good creation. But humanity rejected God, and ever since we have lived in rebellion against him and in conflict with each other. But God chose Abraham and his family to be the beginning of a new humanity. He rescued this people from slavery and made a covenant through which they could relate to him and display his glory to the world. When they persistently rejected God, he promised a remnant who would continue the promise of a people who know God. He promised a new covenant bringing forgiveness for sin and his Law written on their hearts. Ultimately Jesus was that faithful remnant. He died for his people to redeem God's new humanity. And he rose as the first among many who would enjoy new life in a new creation. God is now gathering his people through the mission of the church and will present them, drawn from all nations, as the perfected bride of his Son."

The invitation implicit in this story is not simply to an individual relationship with God (though that is one implication). The invitation is to become part of the new people of God, the bride of Christ. It suggests a spirituality with a much more communal orientation. Here is a spirituality in which we grasp the amazing dimensions of Christ's love "together with all the saints" (Ephesians 3:18). We model and embody God's love for one another (1 John 4:12). *I* have a relationship with God because *we* have a relationship with God. There are *persons* of God because there is a *people* of God.

What does this mean in practice? Here are three suggestions.

First, it means we should prioritize prayer with others over prayer alone. It is when two agree that Christ promises to answer prayer and when two or three are gathered that Christ promises to be with us (Matthew 18:19–20). Not only does this reflect the communal nature of our relationship with God, but experience suggests

149

that for most people it is easier. On my own my thoughts are soon distracted. Praying with other people somehow seems to sustain my concentration. I meet each weekday morning at 8:30 A.M. to pray briefly with another Christian. Other people I know read the Bible and pray in the car as they commute together to work. We also encourage people to pray together in the midst of ordinary life. When you are talking about a problem, turn that conversation into prayer. When you are celebrating a success, turn that conversation into praise. I also pray alone for two reasons. First, I need to pray more often than just the times when I am with other Christians. Second, I still fear other people's opinion much too freely to disclose my heart before them in prayer. It should not be like this, but it is. And so there are times when I need to be more honest with God than I can manage to be in the presence of other people. But I do not rate time alone in prayer over time together in prayer.

Second, we must not separate our relationship with God from our relationship with others. In Isaiah 58, Matthew 5:23–24, Matthew 6:14–15, and 1 Peter 3:7 God says he will not answer prayer. In each case the problem is not sin against God. Sin against God is no barrier to prayer if we are truly repentant. Indeed, we run back to God in prayer to confess our sin and find forgiveness in the gospel. No, in each case the problem is sin against other people (the poor, our Christian family, those who have wronged us, our wife). Sin against others requires us to be first reconciled with them.

Third, we need to exhort and encourage one another daily. Hebrews 3:12–13 says, "See to it, brothers, that none of you has a sinful, unbelieving heart that turns away from the living God. But encourage one another daily, as long as it is called Today, so that none of you may be hardened by sin's deceitfulness." Our hearts are never far from sin, unbelief, hardening, and deception. To persevere we need people who will encourage us, and we need them to encourage us daily (see also Hebrews 10:23–25). The living, active word of God does its heart-softening work through gospel people reminding one another daily of gospel grace. We need to create church cultures in which it is normal and expected for everyone lovingly to confront and persuade everyone. As William Lane says, "The avoidance of apostasy demands not simply individual vigilance but the constant care of each member of the community for one another."[2] Sin is deceitful (v. 13). It never presents itself as sin. It creeps up on us, camouflaged and reasonable: "Of course you have a right to be angry after what they did." "Of course you ought to sleep together since you're planning to get married." "Of course you should have a drink with that man—you need some of the appreciation your husband never gives you." Often we are the last to notice its deceit, but others can and often do. That is why being part of a gospel community is so vital.

This community spirituality clearly requires a certain level of relationship. We need to be sharing our lives. We need to be with other Christians "daily." We need friendships that are real, open, and intimate. We need to give one another license to dig into our lives and challenge our hearts. We need leaders who foster this culture by giving and receiving this daily exhortation, who lead not only from their pulpits but with their lives. The word of God needs not only to be central to church life but thoroughly to pervade every aspect of it.

10

THEOLOGY

A HUNDRED YEARS AGO Martin Kähler argued that mission was "the mother of theology." The New Testament writers did not have the leisure to research and reflect. They wrote, as it were, in emergency situations. It was the church's missionary encounter with the world that created the impetus to do theology. In this chapter we want to paint a vision for theology that takes seriously the Christian gospel, both as a word from God and a word for the world, and the Christian community. So central are these concerns that they actually define true theology and differentiate it from that which is false.

WORD-CENTERED THEOLOGY

Theology has been called "the study of God." But theology is so unlike any other discipline that it ought not to be considered in the same category. In biology, for example, the biologist studies the plant and deduces information through analysis and research. The plant itself is the passive object of dispassionate scientific scrutiny. God, however, is never a passive object!

All theology or discourse about God proceeds on the basis that God has revealed himself. The initiative is his alone. Our knowledge of God is dependent upon his own self-disclosure. So theology is not philosophy: it is neither speculative in nature nor esoteric in content.

All theology must be the fruit of serious engagement with the Bible. Theology, properly understood, is an encounter with the living God in his word.

Furthermore, God's self-disclosure in Christ the Word and in the word of the Bible is that which scrutinizes us. As we examine the light, the light exposes our flaws and reveals an alternative, authentic reality. It is in learning about God that we come to know ourselves. Herman Bavinck, in his inaugural address as professor of systematic theology at the Free University of Amsterdam, said, "A theologian is a person who makes bold to speak about God because he speaks out of God and through God. To profess theology is to do holy work. It is a priestly ministration in the house of the Lord. It is itself a service of worship, a consecration of mind and heart to the honour of his name."[1]

In his final letter to Timothy, Paul reminds him of the Scriptures he was taught as a child. Timothy faces false teachers whom Paul describes as "evil men and impostors" who "go from bad to worse, deceiving and being deceived" (3:13). In contrast, Timothy is to continue in what he has learned (3:14; see also 1:13). His point of reference is the Holy Scriptures, for these alone give the wisdom that leads to salvation in Christ (3:15). All other teaching consists of "foolish and stupid arguments" (2:23). So Timothy is to apply himself diligently to the study of the Scriptures as "a workman who does not need to be ashamed and who correctly handles the word of truth" (2:15). Timothy's task is essentially simple, if not always easy: as a leader of God's people, teaching them truth and protecting them from error, Timothy is to work hard at studying the Bible.

In contrast to the faulty doctrine and corrupt lives of the false teachers, the Scriptures show how health and sanity are to be found only in Christ. The Scriptures make us wise for salvation: all the benefits bestowed on believers by God are understood through his word. Just as breath forms my thoughts into words that you can hear, so God breathes out through the Spirit, and the result is the Bible. The followers of the false teachers are "always learning but never able to acknowledge the truth" (3:7). In contrast, as Calvin puts it, "The Lord, when he gave us the Scriptures, did not intend either to gratify our curiosity . . . or to give occasion for chatting and talking, but to do us good. Therefore the right use of Scripture must always tend to what is profitable."[2] The man of God is equipped by the word of God for every good work because Scripture "is useful for teaching, rebuking, correcting and training in righteousness" (3:16). Because it leads to salvation, the Bible gives us truth both to believe and to live. "Scripture contains the perfect rule of a good and happy life."[3] This is why Paul is convinced Timothy has all he needs to conduct his ministry, rebut false teachers, and equip the saints for godliness.

MISSION-CENTERED THEOLOGY

Because theology is always the fruit of engagement with the Bible, it is not the preserve of the academic, nor is its pursuit confined to academic institutions. Theology is the task of the local church. If, as Bavinck claims, "a theologian is a person who makes bold to speak about God," then every believer is a theologian in the fullest sense of that word. As we speak the truth about God to the world and one another, we speak as theologians because God is the subject of our conversation.

Theology is also the task of the church because the only theology that matters and is worthy of the name is practical theology. Theology is the stuff of life. Theology is a service of worship that extends over the whole of life. The wife who submits to her husband as to Christ and the husband who loves his wife as Christ loved the church are theologians. They are people who know the word of God and allow that word to transform them in lives of humble, self-forgetting service.

Meaningful theology needs to take place primarily in the routine life of the people of God. It needs to be discourse that engages with life and arises out of life. The supposed medieval concern about the number of angels on a pinhead may illustrate all that is silly about "professional" theology, but a cursory glance at even some evangelical theological journals reveals contemporary discussions that are no less obscure. They may sound scholarly and impressive, but they is fundamentally sterile and too often irrelevant. Their irrelevance is compounded when the discourses are not driven by a desire to live life to the glory of God.

Theology must be in the service of the church and its mission. Authentic theology must be shaped by what we might call a missionary hermeneutic. Theology divorced from this context is essentially barren, self-referential, and indulgent. David Bosch says, "Just as the church ceases to be church if it is not missionary, theology ceases to be theology if it loses its missionary character. . . . We are in need of a missiological agenda for theology rather than just a theological agenda for mission; for theology, rightly understood, has no reason to exist other than critically to accompany the *missio Dei*."[4]

I find time and again that talking to non-Christians forces me to take my theology to another level. "I pray," says Paul to Philemon, "that you may be active in sharing your faith, so that you will have a full understanding of every good thing we have in Christ" (v. 6). Unbelievers are not satisfied with the pat answers and unexplained terminology that Christians all too often readily accept.

The missionary task of crossing cultures presents particular opportunities for the renewal of theology. "Every culture makes possible a certain approach to the gospel that brings to light certain of its aspects that in other cultures may remain less visible or even hidden."[5] We necessarily express our theology in cultural ways. That is right. But it also has dangers. We can begin to confuse gospel truth with cultural prejudices. Communicating the gospel cross-culturally and across subcultures causes us to reflect on how much of our Christian practice arises from the gospel and how much from our own culture. Mission is the opportunity to rethink which elements of what we believe do belong to the gospel and which in fact belong to our culture.

It seems incongruous that in the classic divisions of systematic theology there is usually no place for mission! If mission is included at all, it is as a subset of *church*. But we need more than a theology of mission that sits alongside our theology of the church, of salvation, of Christ, and so on. We need to rethink all of theology in missionary terms because every situation is a missionary situation. We need a missional approach to doctrine, to biblical studies, to church history, to ethics, to pastoral care, and so on. David Smith says:

> It scarcely needs to be said that biblical studies would be released from captivity to an arid, purely technical approach to the text of Scripture. For example, how is it possible to avoid the missionary implication of the Song of Songs in a culture which has forgotten the meaning of pure love; or the apologetic value of Ecclesiastes in an age of nihilism? Does not the message of Job leap from the page with extraordinary relevance in a century that has witnessed the sufferings of Auschwitz and Belsen? When one moves to more familiar territory, say, the book of Psalms, or the prophets, not to mention the parables of Jesus, we have our hands full of material which is spiritual dynamite in our contemporary world.[6]

Restoring biblical theology to its true home in the believing, missionary community is at once a far more accessible and a far more demanding enterprise. It demands of us that our Bible teaching should always look to explore the missionary implications of a passage—to make the truth plain and to make it real. To that end we need to explore how the text speaks to contemporary culture. At its most basic level, an integral part of the preparation process is thinking through how to articulate the truths being considered to a non-Christian.

It also means that when issues arise in our churches and ministry, time should be taken to reflect on them theologically. They often present real opportunities to move forward in theological understanding. And without this theological reflection we will be driven by pragmatism or tradition. As theologians together, our "subject" should be exploring the missiological implications of all theology in every aspect of the life of the local church and in every detail of the lives of believers.

Theology must address the issues that arise from our involvement in mission. Mission sets the theological agenda. Our involvement in practice raises questions. The job of theology is to pick up those questions and provide biblical reflection upon them. But that is not enough. Theology must not only *reflect* on action; it must also *lead* to action. The result of theology should be mission.

COMMUNITY-CENTERED THEOLOGY

The evangelical Anabaptists provide a helpful working model of this approach with their commitment to "a community hermeneutic." The gospel community was an integral part of interpreting the Bible and doing theology. John Howard Yoder says, "It is a basic novelty in the discussion of hermeneutics to say that a text is best understood in a congregation."[7] The text is only properly understood when believers are gathered together to discover what the word has to say to them, with each person contributing his or her own perspective and experiences.

There are a number of dimensions to this understanding. First, most of the New Testament was written to gospel communities. This suggests that the best context in which to understand them is a gospel community. The Old Testament, too, was for the most part the product of a community identity, a community called to be a light to the nations. Bible interpretation is not just about me and my Bible. It is about God's word to his people, a people with a responsibility toward the world. Both accounts of the Ten Commandments, for example, are set in the context of Israel's call to be a royal priesthood mediating the knowledge of God to the nations (Exodus 19:5–6) and a community that modeled life under God's rule (Deuteronomy 4:5–8). If you want to understand the role of the Law and its implications today, you need to recognize that the Law was given in the context of the call to be a missionary community.

Second, one of the issues the Reformation raised was how to decide between competing interpretations of the Bible. The Catholic answer was that the hierarchy of the church decided: the Pope was the ultimate authority. The Protestant answer was that every believer decides: every man is his own pope. In practice, this developed at times into the popery of scholarship with the academy determining the true interpretation of the Bible. It ran to seed in theological liberalism with human scholarship sitting in judgment on the word of God.

From the beginning the Anabaptist response was to say that the community of believers determines together the interpretation of Scripture. They held that Scripture was plain and that the gathered believers could understand the Scriptures. The Anabaptists spoke of "the Rule of Paul," a reference to 1 Corinthians 14:29: "Two or three prophets should speak, and the others should weigh carefully what is said."

Third, the hermeneutics of community is closely related to another important idea—the hermeneutics of obedience. There is, the Anabaptists argued, a close connection between understanding the Bible and obeying the Bible, between knowledge and discipleship. Anabaptists like Hans Denck and Hans Hut used to say that true knowledge of God cannot be achieved simply from reading the Bible. Hans Denck said, "No man can know Christ unless he follows after him in life." The readiness to obey Christ's words is prerequisite to understanding them. And if discipleship was necessary for understanding, then a discipling community was necessary for understanding. The Christian community is the context in which commitment to obedience is nurtured and maintained, and so it is the context in which theology must be done.

In Ephesians 4:11–16 Paul affirms the role of teachers but suggests their role is "to prepare God's people for works of service, so that the body of Christ may be built up until we all reach unity in the faith and in the knowledge of the Son of God and become mature, attaining to the whole measure of the fullness of Christ" (vv. 12–13). Notice that we reach "knowledge of the Son of God" together. Our understanding progresses as we grow together. My growth as a Christian is in some sense linked to your growth. Only together do we attain maturity.

A number of our congregations have a weekly teachers' meeting. All those who teach the Bible get together to look at the passage a couple of weeks in advance. We work on the text together and think about its application. It is a great context in which to teach people to handle the Bible. People learn hermeneutics not through an artificial methodology but through the repeated practice of working on the text of Scripture. It is also a creative way to study. Most people think best by talking things through with others. So the best method of preparation for them is probably not to sit alone with a pile of books. Time and again we find that we spark one another off, gaining a level of understanding far beyond anything we might have achieved individually. It also means the community as a whole grapples with the text. The main thing that prevents us from understanding the Bible aright is not a lack of hermeneutical skills but our sin. Our sin warps our understanding because we all tend toward self-justification. Studying the text with other people reduces the impact of sin on our thinking.

The teachers' meeting is only the beginning of the process. We include group interaction so that the community as a whole wrestles with the meaning and implications of the text. We encourage people to continue the conversation into the week and to walk with one another as we apply it to our lives. And this is only half the picture. It represents the movement of Bible to life or word to world. We also want to move from world to word, encouraging people to reflect biblically in the context of the community on issues raised by life and ministry. In our team meetings, for example, we invite people to raise questions for the group to think through together.

THE THEOLOGY OF THE ACADEMY AND THE THEOLOGY OF THE CHURCH

A significant part of the problem behind academic theology and biblical scholarship is the way in which it is, all too often, self-referential. Professional theologians often write about and for other professional theologians. In the New Testament, church leaders were responsible for guarding the flock from error (Acts 20:28–31). They were, if you like, theologians-in-residence within the congregation. We have often moved this function of guarding from error into the academy, but this is a dangerous place for it to reside. We ought not to underestimate the influence of the metaphorical concept of "home." If the theologian's "home" is academia, then approval from other "family" members will be important. This can be painfully illustrated by the lives of former evangelicals who pursued academic careers with noble ambitions, yet sadly ended up a considerable distance from their evangelical roots. Theology does share certain conventions with other academic disciplines. But if the primary "home" of theology is the believing community, it will more likely be earthed in life and will more likely remain evangelical.

Some claim we need those who are intellectually "on a par" with academic theologians in our universities to engage with contemporary theological issues. To a large extent, however, contemporary theology is pursued by people who make no pretense of being "Christian," working in non-confessional institutions. If true theology is the fruit of engagement with the Bible set in the context of the local church, then much of what passes for theology is not theology at all. Why do we allow such people to set the agenda?

Non-believing theologians are part of a culture that looks at life from the standpoint of unbelief, and this unbelief is an issue of the heart more than a problem of the intellect. Don Cupitt, a "theologian" who rejects a personal, objective deity, says, "First, I must have the freedom of action I need if I am to follow the course of life and habits of action that will make me the person I want to be; secondly, I must be autonomous in the sense of being able to make my own rules and impose them on myself; and thirdly, the morality I actually adopt must itself be autonomous in the secondary sense of being intrinsically authoritative."[8] Underlying Cupitt's rejection of divine revelation is a rejection of divine rule in favor of individual autonomy. Cupitt attacks, sometimes with venomous language, what he characterizes as other-worldly, life-denying religion. In the name of Cupitt's alternative, this-worldly, life-affirming worldview, "today, obedience is sin."[9]

Such objections to the gospel will not be settled by clever arguments. As Augustine said, "Unless you believe, you will not understand." The gospel of Christ crucified is always a foolish and offensive message. No matter how much "theology-speak" we use, the gospel requires that we eventually come to the crux issue, and at that point our academic credibility is always lost!

Please understand that this is not a plea for dumbing down the truth of God, nor for despising theology per se. It is a critique of professional theology removed from the furnace of life and not hammered into shape on the anvil of the local church. As Calvin says, doctrine is an affair "not of the tongue, but of life. It is not apprehended by the understanding and memory alone, as other disciplines are, but it is received only when it possesses the whole soul, and finds a seat and resting place in the inmost affection of the heart. . . . It must enter our heart and pass into our daily living, and so transform us into itself that it may not be unfruitful for us."[10]

11

APOLOGETICS

WE WILL CONTINUE OUR discussion with the topic of apologetics.

THE MESSAGE OF THE CROSS AND THE LIMITS OF RATIONAL APOLOGETICS

Most modern Christian apologetics is a response to the Enlightenment and its apparent rejection of Christian revelation in favor of rationalism. The Enlightenment was the intellectual movement spanning the eighteenth, nineteenth, and twentieth centuries that shaped modernity, the worldview of our modern world. It is often known as "the age of reason." Rejecting the supposed superstition of religion, it was and is supremely confident in the ability of human reason to discover truth. René Descartes's famous dictum "I think therefore I am" was a defining insight for the Enlightenment. Beliefs can only be accepted on the basis of reason, not on the authority of priest, sacred texts, or tradition. Private faith was acceptable, but public life and discourse should be conducted on the basis of reason. Whereas religion divided communities, reasoned debate, it was argued, would in time lead to a shared interpretation of the world. Through reason humanity could overcome the problems that plague humanity. Nature could be conquered by the natural sciences, and human nature could be perfected by the social sciences.

Not everyone embraced this onward march of reason. The Romantic movement rebelled against its cold embrace. Poets like William Blake and William Wordsworth feared a mechanized, rationalistic world and championed instead the sensibilities of the human spirit. Johann Wolfgang von Goethe, another philosopher-poet, said, "Existence divided by human reason leaves a remainder."[1] But Romanticism remains a movement within the Enlightenment, for humanity is still at the center. Reason is replaced by experience, but humanity is still the judge of truth.

Its rejection of the Bible as a source of divine revelation brought the Enlightenment into confrontation with biblical Christianity. Some Enlightenment thinkers were atheists, but many were deists. Like Matthew Tindal in his book *Christianity as Old as the Creation* (1730), they looked at the evidence of the world around them and concluded there was a god, albeit one who was not intimately involved in his world. What they were agreed on was that divine revelation could not form a basis for public knowledge.

Many within the church capitulated to this "progressive" view, conceding ground to the rationalists. As a child in school assemblies, I was told that the feeding of the five thousand occurred not through a divine miracle but because the crowd were shamed into sharing their secret food by the boy's willingness to share his five loaves and two fish. The miracles of the Bible were discounted and "demythologized." Human beings no longer saw themselves under the authority of God's word. Now they judged the truth or otherwise of the Bible. The supernatural was stripped out of Christianity in the vain hope of making it credible. But in fact the leftover dead husk was not worth believing.

Other Christians responded to this assault on biblical truth by retreating into a ghetto. In the Enlightenment worldview the public truth of science, politics, economics, culture, and education was based on reason and observation. Religious faith was a private matter. So Christians found they could happily practice their faith and maintain their orthodoxies within their own circles as long as they did not bring their religion into the public discourse.

Some Christians, however, engaged with the modern worldview. They took it on, challenging it on its own terms. They defended the Christian faith through rational discourse. The Enlightenment's age of reason spawned rational apologetics. Some believed that since "all truth is God's truth," rational inquiry would inevitably lead people toward God rather than away from him. Christians could use reason to prove God, just as Thomas Aquinas had used his cosmological arguments to argue the existence of God in the medieval period. Others were more circumspect. They believed Christians could demonstrate the integrity and rationality of the Christian faith even if they could not "prove" God. Christians could show that faith was not a "leap in the dark" but had its own rational coherence. But they could not prove faith in God in a logically compelling way. Faith is still faith and not the proving ground of rational analysis. However ambitious this approach, it countered the perceived conflict between reason and revelation through rational argument.

This reading of the history of Western thought has been challenged by Stephen Williams in his book *Revelation and Reconciliation*. Williams argues that modern atheism has its roots elsewhere. The rejection of revelation is only a symptom of an underlying problem. The real problem is the rejection of the idea of reconciliation and all that is implicit in that idea—moral accountability to the Creator, human helplessness, and reconciliation with God through a substitutionary sacrifice. The underlying issue was not a rejection of the *possibility* of revelation but a rejection of the *actuality* of revelation. In other words, the underlying problem is not revelation per se but what is revealed—our need for a Savior. "Western atheism may be understood as a spiritual movement of the soul as well as an intellectual movement of the mind."[2] The Enlightenment is better understood as a movement toward human autonomy or freedom from the claims of God and the proud rejection of human helplessness. Williams does not say the rejection of revelation was insignificant but that we must also see alongside and underlying it the rejection of reconciliation. Consider the following quotation:

> It has gradually become clear to me what every great philosophy has hitherto been: a confession on the part of its author and a kind of involuntary and unconscious memoir; moreover that the moral (or immoral) intentions in every philosophy have every time constituted the real germ of life out of which the entire plant has grown. To explain how a philosopher's most remote metaphysical assertions have actually been arrived at, it is always well (and wise) to ask oneself first: what morality does this (does *he*) aim at? I accordingly do not believe a 'drive to knowledge' to be the father of philosophy, but that another drive has, here as elsewhere, only employed knowledge (and false knowledge!) as a tool.[3]

This is a quotation from the philosopher Friedrich Nietzsche, in many ways the supreme manifestation of modernist thinking. But, as Nietzsche recognizes with characteristic honesty, all philosophy, however rational, is ultimately a justification for the way we want to live our lives. And modern people want to live their lives without God. So they construct a worldview in which God is either marginal (deism) or nonexistent (atheism). Aldous Huxley says:

> I had motives for not wanting the world to have a meaning; and consequently assumed that it had none, and was able without any difficulty to find satisfying reasons for this assumption. . . . The philosopher who finds no meaning in the world is not concerned exclusively with a problem in pure metaphysics; he is also concerned to prove that there is no valid reason why he personally should not do as he wants to do. For myself, as, no doubt, for most of my contemporaries, the philosophy of meaninglessness was essentially an instrument of liberation . . . from a certain system of morality. We objected to the morality because it interfered with our sexual freedom; we objected to the political and economic system because it was unjust. The supporters of these systems claimed that in some way they embodied the meaning (a Christian meaning, they insisted) of the world. There was one admirably simple method of confuting these people and at the same time justifying ourselves in our political and erotic revolt: we could deny that the world had any meaning whatsoever.[4]

The movement is not from metaphysics to morality, from atheism to human autonomy. It is not that we reluctantly concluded that there is no God and then worked out how we should live in such a world. No, the movement is from morality to metaphysics.[5] We want to be free from God's rule, and so we construct a worldview in which God is absent. As Nietzsche puts it, "God is dead. . . . And we have killed him."[6]

This should come as no surprise to readers of the Bible. The "fool" in Psalm 14 who says in his heart, "There is no God" is not ignorant. "They are corrupt, their deeds are vile; there is no one who does good," says the psalmist (v. 1). What prevents us from knowing God is our rebellion against him. Paul says, "For since the creation of the world God's invisible qualities—his eternal power and divine nature—have been clearly seen, being understood from what has been made, so that men are without excuse" (Romans 1:20). At first sight this seems to suggest that we can know God through observation and reason. But Paul goes on, "For although they knew God, they neither glorified him as God nor gave thanks to him, but their thinking became futile and their foolish hearts were darkened" (v. 21). The problem is that people "suppress the truth by their wickedness" (v. 18). The light of God's revelation has come into the world in the person of Jesus Christ. But "men loved darkness instead of light because their deeds were evil." A person rejects the light "for fear that his deeds will be exposed" (John 3:19–20). The problem is not that we *cannot* know God. The problem is that we *will* not know God. It is a problem of the heart rather than the head.

Consider the following statement: "Language seems so skilfully crafted that it appears to be the work of a master architect—and yet its complex structure must somehow have arisen of its own accord."[7] The illogic is glaring. Ockham's razor, the age-old philosophical rule of thumb, says that the simplest explanation is to be preferred. If language is so skillfully crafted that it seems to be the work of a master architect, then the simplest explanation must surely be that there is a master architect. But the rejection of the existence of a master architect is a presupposition before the argument can ever get underway. The point is not that the complexity of language definitively proves the existence of God. The point is that people reject God not because of reason but as a presupposition and sometimes despite reason.

This is the significance of Blaise Pascal's famous challenge. The seventeenth-century philosopher invited people to consider the following wager: If you "bet" on the existence of God and find at death he does not exist, then you have lost very little. But if you "bet" instead on God's nonexistence and discover at death that God does exist, then you have lost everything eternally. His point was not to demonstrate the profitability of "betting" on God but to expose the unbeliever's innate hostility to God. Betting against God is contrary to self-interest and is counter-rational because it is driven by deeper impulses than reason. Graham Tomlin comments:

> The Wager is designed to blow the myth of neutrality out of the water. . . . Pascal has brought his interlocutor to realize that he is an unbeliever not because Christianity is inherently implausible, but because he simply does not want to believe. It is not lack of proofs, but a deeply irrational distaste for the foolishness of Christianity which prevents his conversion . . . "your inability to believe derives from your passions," rather than from any intellectual difficulty. The real origin of this decision not to believe is not solid intellectual objection, or the inherent irrationality of Christianity, but an irrational and unfounded prejudice, based on an inability to see the truth of Christian faith. The problem is not lack of evidence but sin.[8]

At the Fall, says Pascal, love for God was replaced by self-love. This self-love infected all human existence, including our ability to reason. It is this lack of true love that corrupts our ability to know God and understand reality. As Augustine had argued, our self-love blinds us to the love of God. The primary question in the forefront of the Enlightenment was the question of epistemology—that is, how we can know the truth. But Pascal "insists that the essential problem is not primarily epistemological [to do with knowledge], but soteriological [to do with salvation]. It is not a failure to understand God, it is failure to love him."[9]

Corresponding to human blindness is God's hiddenness. God hides himself from those who would know him without loving him. Pascal glories in the obscurity of Christianity, its "folly" as Paul describes it in 1 Corinthians 1. This obscurity is what we should expect from a God who hides himself from those who have no desire to love him. The revelation of God in Christ is ambiguous. Only through the gift of faith do we discern the presence of God in the shame of the cross. The cross is the ultimate barrier to rational apologetics. Indeed, if we should succeed in rationally proving Christianity, we would thereby disprove it, for we would disprove the folly of the cross. Christianity is folly because God has made it folly to hide himself from those who would not love him. Knowledge of God turns on the cross. The cross is the revelation of God to those disposed to love God, but it hides God from those disposed to reject his reign. The Puritan Richard Sibbes said, "Those that can bring their hearts to delight in Christ know most his ways. . . . Love is the best entertainer of truth."[10]

Martin Luther argues in a similar vein. He developed his "theology of the cross" in the Heidelberg Disputation in 1518 through a series of theses and explanations. Thesis 19 states, "He is not worth calling a theologian who seeks to interpret the invisible things of God on the basis of the things that have been created." The question Luther is addressing is this: How can we know God? There are some visible things humanity could look at—creation, spiritual experiences, miracles. But Luther says they do not reveal God. Or rather, they reveal something of God, but this kind of knowledge puffs people up so that they never get beyond it. This knowledge is never enough for a man, nor could it benefit him. People think they have knowledge, but they do not; they are fools.

Is God then unknowable? If we cannot know God through what is visible, can we know him at all? Luther's answer is that

God is known through what is contrary. He is known in a hidden way. God's invisible attributes are revealed in suffering and the cross—glory in shame, wisdom in folly, power in weakness, victory in defeat. God is known through the message of the cross. The theology of the cross stems from Luther's understanding of righteousness and justification. Luther's great realization was that God justified sinners. God declares those who are unjust to be just. And Luther realized that this being so, human notions of justice could never lead us to understand God's justice. God's justice is revealed in the opposite of justice—in the justification of sinners.

If knowledge of God could be obtained from what is visible (creation, spiritual experiences, miracles), that would lead to pride. So God determined to be known through suffering so that he would be hidden from all those who exalt themselves. Only someone who has had all the spirit taken out of him and has been broken can know God. Elsewhere Luther says "humility" or even "humiliation" is the precondition for knowing God. Only someone who is humbled or crushed before God can truly know him. The theologians of glory pursue wisdom, experience, and miracles, and they say that suffering is bad. But the theologian of the cross values suffering as that through which God is revealed. Knowledge of God is not found through human wisdom, powers, or achievements but in the foolishness of the cross.

Knowing one another always involves humility. I need to approach others with humility because I am dependent on their disclosing themselves to me. This is all the more so when another is superior in some way. If I wanted to know the British monarch or the American President, I would have to approach them humbly, courteously, respectfully. I would have to accept a relationship on their terms. I could not "investigate" them from a position of superiority. Even in the sciences you have to be humble before data, not imposing a view but being ready to accept what investigation reveals. Knowing God also involves humility. We come to him on his terms, dependent on him to disclose himself.

It requires faith to recognize God in the absence of God, to recognize victory in defeat, to recognize glory in shame. God is known only by faith. And because this requires faith, it is an act of grace. We do not contribute to our salvation—it is all God's doing. It is the same for our knowledge of God. We do not contribute to our knowledge of God—it is all God's doing. God reveals himself in a hidden way in order to safeguard the graciousness of revelation. "I praise you, Father, Lord of heaven and earth," says Jesus, "because you have hidden these things from the wise and learned, and revealed them to little children" (Matthew 11:25). We do not know God because we are cleverer than other people or have greater spiritual insight or have spent more time in contemplation. We know God because God graciously reveals himself to us in the message of the cross. We know the hidden God through the grace of God. God is known through the message of the cross—power in weakness, glory in shame, wisdom in folly. Hear Sibbes again:

> Where Christ by his Spirit as a prophet teaches, he likewise as a king by his Spirit subdueth the heart to obedience of what is taught. This is that teaching which is promised of God, when not only the brain, but the heart itself, is taught: when men do not only know what they should do, but are taught the very doing of it; they are not only taught that they should love, fear, and obey, but they are taught love itself, and fear and obedience itself. . . . The same Spirit that enlighteneth the mind, inspireth gracious inclinations into the will and affections, and infuseth strength into the whole man.[11]

We begin to see the relevance of the theology of the cross when we start to consider what forms a theology of glory takes today. Liberalism can be labeled a theology of glory, for it argues that God is known through human reason. Sacramentalism claims we encounter God through the symbols and rituals of the church. Creation spiritualities can also take the form of theologies of glory, whether it is the sentiment expressed in "nearer to God in a garden" or the more developed theology of someone like Matthew

Fox. Power evangelism, too, looks for the revelation of God in acts of power, arguing that miracles are an essential part of effective mission. And mysticism says that God is known through spiritual experiences or contemplative exercises.

All of these are alive and well in modified forms within evangelicalism. This is why Luther's theology of the cross remains so significant today. How do we know God? Not primarily through mystical insight or theological wisdom or supernatural visions or words of knowledge or the beauty of creation. We know God through the message of the cross. How do we know the power of God? Not primarily through rational argument or healing miracles or political influence or spiritual disciplines or media presence or alternative worship or managerial skill or megachurches or inspirational leaders or sociological theories. Human wisdom does not recognize divine wisdom. We know the power of God through the message of the cross.

This does not mean there is no place for rational apologetics. But it means that such approaches must be less ambitious. Their role is not to persuade unbelievers. The role of rational apologetics is to demonstrate that unbelief is a problem of the heart rather than a problem of the head. People may claim that the obstacle to faith is the problem of suffering or the implausibility of miracles or the existence of other religions. The role of rational apologetics is to show that these are not the real causes of unbelief. It is to strip away the excuses and expose rebellious hearts.

Moreover, as experience so often demonstrates, what counts is commonly not the answer we give but the gracious and respectful manner in which we treat questioning people. As someone wrote to me recently, "I was struck by the testimony of one non-Christian after doing a Bible study with Andy. He talked a lot about how kind and patient Andy was. At first I thought this was less than ideal—after all, the gospel is not about Andy! But reflecting on it, the fact that the gospel was heard was probably due to Andy being respectful, approachable, sacrificial, and loving. It certainly gave the message credibility."

THE MESSAGE OF THE CROSS AND THE LIMITS OF POSTMODERNISM

Modernity was premised on the assumption that humanity could discover the truth through rational inquiry. Differences were due to varying degrees of ignorance or irrationality. Over time humanity would come to a common understanding of the truth through scientific exploration and rational debate.

Postmodernity rightly rebels against this notion. It rejects it because human beings are finite and fallible. Postmodernity rightly discerns that truth-claims are often as much a function of power as of knowledge. In this it mirrors the Christian understanding that rebellious hearts are more an impediment to understanding than ignorant minds. Postmodernity suspects that claims to absolute truth are just ways of exercising power over people. In its more radical forms it questions the whole notion of absolute truth. More often it questions whether human beings can legitimately claim to know absolute truth. We are left with different perspectives, all of which are equally valid or whose validity cannot be verified. This rejection of truth did not come out of nowhere. The suspicion is that truth is a function of power. Truth is shaped by those in power to maintain their status and wealth. Inside the glove of truth is the fist of power.

The response of some Christians to the claim that truth is corrupted by power is to deny the problem or to claim that the situation is not too bad. In part that is because many Christians belong to social groups that benefit from the status quo. The received wisdom works in their favor. They are happy to leave establishment truth unchallenged, whether it is the defense of big business or the myths about asylum seekers or the government line on foreign policy.

But truth *is* corrupted by power. The postmodern case is valid. The problem, however, is that the postmodern solution does not work. The rejection of truth does not work. Truth is rejected as a tool of power, but disregarding truth simply leaves the field open to power. There is nothing left with which to resist power. There is nothing worth fighting for. The pen may or may not be mightier than the sword. But if you take the pen away, you are simply left with the sword. Postmodern people fear that truth-claims are coercive. But if you take truth away you are left with pure coercion.

So if power is to be used properly, we need an authority to which we are all accountable. In Revelation 4 John sees "a door standing open in heaven" (v. 1). He takes us behind the scenes of history, and we see there the throne of God surrounded by all the splendor of heaven. The chapter ends with the cry, "You are worthy, our Lord and God, to receive glory and honor and power, for you created all things, and by your will they were created and have their being" (v. 11). The ultimate truth of God and power of God provide a critique and a criteria to measure all other truth-claims. The book of Revelation was written to Christians living under the power of the Roman Empire. This was "eternal Rome" who ruled the world. Graffiti found in Rome reads, "Rome—your power will never end." We do not know whether it was the proud claim of a beneficiary of Roman power or the despairing cry of one of her victims. But John reveals that Rome's power *will* end. It is Jesus, not Rome, who is "the First and the Last" (1:17). There is a power over and above Roman power. There is a truth over and above Roman propaganda. To resist the misuse of truth by the powerful, we do not need less truth—we need more truth. We need to rediscover the ultimate truth—the lordship of God.

In Revelation 5 John sees the occupant of the throne of heaven. And what he sees is "a Lamb, looking as if it had been slain" (vv. 5–6). The Empire of the Lamb is not coercive, for it is built on the sacrificial death of its King. Our King is the king who gives his life for his people. The truth we proclaim is not a function of coercive power but of sacrificial love.

Who rules from the throne? Who can open the scrolls of history? Who is the ultimate authority? It is the Lamb. It is the One who has been slain. It is the One who gave his life for us. This is the truth that sets us free. We can know God and therefore know absolute truth because God has revealed himself in his Son and through his Spirit. And as we have seen, this is not an arrogant claim because it does not depend on our intelligence but upon God's grace. The revelation of God in the cross destroys human pretensions. There is no room to boast.

THE COMMUNITY OF THE CROSS AND RELATIONAL APOLOGETICS

So people reject the knowledge of God not because they *cannot* know God, but because they *will* not know him. At root it is not an intellectual problem of the head but a relational problem of the heart. This has profound implications for apologetics. The Danish philosopher Søren Kierkegaard says:

> People try to persuade us that the objections against Christianity spring from doubt. The objections against Christianity spring from insubordination, the dislike of obedience, rebellion against all authority. As a result people have hitherto been beating the air in the struggle against objections, because they have fought intellectually with doubt instead of fighting morally with rebellion.[12]

Modern Christianity has developed a rational apologetic. We engage modern society with rational proofs of God's existence. We provide scientific data to defend divine creation. We have developed logical responses to the questions raised by suffering. All of these presuppose that modern people find the Christian faith intellectually weak. But the problem is not an intellectual problem. The problem is hearts that refuse to live under God's reign. We reject God. It is a relational problem. And if it is a relational problem, it requires a relational apologetic.

What will commend the gospel are lives lived in obedience to the gospel and a community life that reflects God's triune community of love. People will not believe until they are genuinely open to exploring the truth about God. They become open as they see that it is good to know God. And they see that it is good to know God as they see the love of the Christian community. As Francis Schaeffer said, "Our relationship with each other is the criterion the world uses to judge whether our message is truthful. Christian community is the ultimate apologetic."[13]

As we have seen, the missiological paradigm of the Old and New Testaments is that of a community drawing the nations to God. The serpent's lie in Eden was that God's rule was harsh and tyrannical. Believing the lie, humanity rejects God's rule. By rejecting this, we reject the knowledge of God (Romans 1:21). God's people are to model life under the rule of God through obedience to his word. As they do this the nations will see that God's rule brings life and blessing. Chris Wright comments:

> The social shape of Israel . . . was an integral part of what God has called them into existence for. God's message of redemption through Israel was not just verbal; it was visible and tangible. They, the medium, were themselves part of the message. . . . It would be as they lived out the quality of national and social life demanded by the law . . . with its great chords of freedom, justice, love and compassion, that they would function as God's holy priesthood: as a nation, among the nations, for the nations.[14]

Peter takes the language of Exodus 19:4–6 and applies it to the church in 1 Peter 2:9: "You are a chosen people, a royal priesthood, a holy nation, a people belonging to God, that you may declare the praises of him who called you out of darkness into his wonderful light." Israel was given the Law to define what it meant to be a kingdom of priests and a holy nation. As they lived under God's reign expressed through God's word, they would attract the nations to God. Now, says Peter, the church is that kingdom of priests and holy nation. And they, too, are to "live such good lives among the pagans that, though they accuse you of doing wrong, they may see your good deeds and glorify God on the day he visits us" (1 Peter 2:12). Paul tells Titus to teach slaves to live in such a way that they "make the teaching about God our Savior attractive" (Titus 2:10).

Name: Alasdair
Occupation: Part-time supermarket worker
Church: The Crowded House, Abbey

For Alasdair, life is the difference between then and now. Then was six or seven nights out drinking and doing drugs; now is organizing events to promote evangelism opportunities. Then was being disconnected and looking for something more out of life; now is being part of a Christian community and looking to help others.

When Alasdair became a Christian a couple of years ago, his life turned 180 degrees. In a deliberate move he now works part-time in a supermarket. He uses his free hours to meet with and encourage congregation members as well as to plan social events that bring them into contact with people who don't know Jesus. "I call, text, or e-mail, organizing events such as karaoke nights, quiz nights at the pub, or just going to the movies," he says. "I have enough time for work and enough time for those at The Crowded House if they need me."

Besides, Alasdair no longer sees work as just work. Two of his colleagues, John and Rebecca, are Christians, and he spends time encouraging them in their faith. "John and I meet at least once a week outside work," he says. "We encourage each other and see how the Bible helps us cope with our jobs. And we always spend Tuesday lunchtime in the work canteen, so we can create building blocks with the other staff."

Alasdair first heard the gospel through a woman he worked with in a thrift store. By his own admission, he was looking for more friends at the time and feeling as if he wanted to be part of something that mattered. "When I became a Christian I realized that God's family was now my family," he says. "My parents are happy about the change they see in me but don't want it for themselves."

Still there are always the karaoke nights, which his parents come to. This is where they get to meet his other "family." When it comes to singing, Alasdair reckons he's no UK "Pop Idol," but says he'll get up front with the microphone for the sake of the gospel. "You could say I'm singing for Jesus!" he says with a laugh.

The word *apologetics* comes from a Greek word meaning "defense" or "answer." It is the word used in 1 Peter 3:15: "But in your hearts set apart Christ as Lord. Always be prepared to give an answer [*apologia*] to everyone who asks you to give the reason for the hope that you have. But do this with gentleness and respect." Apologetics is answering the questions raised by our lives. This is not simply a matter of lone Christians living godly lives and doing good works. In the Old Testament it was the life of the covenant community that was to function as a light to the nations. And in the New Testament too it is the life of the community that commends the gospel.

In Yann Martel's Booker Prize-winning novel *Life of Pi*, a zoo collection is being transported from India to Canada when the boat sinks. The novel narrates what happens from the perspective of Pi Patel, the zoo owner's son. He describes how he finds himself adrift in a lifeboat with a hyena, a zebra, an orangutan and a 450-pound Royal Bengal tiger. He explains in detail how he and the tiger survive weeks at sea before being washed up on the shore of Mexico. At the end of the novel Pi is prompted by two Japanese insurance investigators to tell another story. In this story he shares the lifeboat with his mother, a cook, and a sailor. It is a story of brutality and murder. Which story is true? Both fit the known facts. In the end Pi asks:

> "Which story do you prefer? Which is the better story, the story with animals or the story without animals?"
> **Mr. Okamoto:** "That's an interesting question . . . "
> **Mr. Chiba:** "The story with animals."
> **Mr. Okamoto:** "Yes. The story with animals is the better story."
> **Pi Patel:** "Thank you. And so it goes with God."
> [Silence][15]

We need to persuade people that our story, the story of God, is true. But they will only explore its truth if we can first persuade them that it might be a better story. We need to address their hearts before we can begin to address the questions in their heads. Commenting on Pascal, Graham Tomlin says:

> For Pascal presenting someone with a list of proofs for Christianity or evidence for faith is probably a waste of time. If someone basically doesn't want to believe, no amount of proof (or proof texts) can ever convince her. And even if she were convinced, then it wouldn't be the Christian God she had come to believe in, but only what Pascal called "the God of the philosophers." The crucial factor in persuading someone to believe, then, is not to present evidence, but first to awaken a desire for God in them. In other words, when commending Christianity to people, "make it attractive, make good men wish it were true, and then show that it is." Such arguments as there are for Christianity can convince those who hope it is true, but will never convince those who don't.[16]

We have a better story than any of the alternatives. We need to awaken a desire for God. We need to make people want Christianity to be true. Then we might be able to persuade them that it is true.

CHILDREN AND YOUNG PEOPLE

AROUND ONE THOUSAND young people walk out of the door of churches in the UK each week, never to return, according to the 1998 English Church Attendance Survey. This ongoing exodus is occurring despite the investment made by churches in youth and children's work. A significant proportion of classified ads in the Christian press for "supported" ministry opportunities are for youth and children's workers. Over the last few decades, churches have taken their responsibility for young people very seriously indeed and have been prepared to put their money where their mouth is. At the very least, this steady stream provides the opportunity to reassess humbly our approach to ministry among children and young people.

When a situation has prevailed for a significant period of time, it is easy to assume that it is a given. It is assumed that "this is the way it is" due to the fact that "this is the way it has always been," which is then only a short step away from asserting that "this is the way it has to be." Even a cursory consideration of changing cultural attitudes toward young people will be adequate to refute this view.

The origins of youth work are difficult to determine with any degree of certainty. The Sunday schools of Robert Raikes could be cited as an example. The Young Men's Christian Association (YMCA) started in 1844. Both of these were a response to social and spiritual needs and began with a clear gospel focus. Toward the end of the nineteenth century, uniformed youth organizations began as a means of evangelism, with groups like Boys' Brigade using a regimental approach to training and evangelism.

The American psychologist G. Stanley Hall began developing theories of adolescence at the turn of the twentieth century. But it was the period immediately after the Second World War and the so-called Baby Boomer Generation that saw both *youth* as a concept and *youth work* really come into their own. It was during this period that teenagers were "invented."

During the 1950s, young people began to be viewed as a social "issue" associated with increased delinquency, the emergence of a so-called youth culture, and specific teenage consumption. These led the British government to appoint the Albemarle Committee in 1960 to look at the question of youth work in England and Wales. This report was a watershed in youth work strategy and provision. Investment in professional youth workers and the development of youth centers followed, encouraging young people to cohere as a distinct group. Ever since, Christian youth work has essentially mirrored this approach and continues to do so.

But the assumptions of the report are increasingly being questioned. Contemporary evidence suggests that the majority of young people do not belong to a distinctive subculture. A case can be argued that "youth," far from identifying a particular age group, is in fact more of an aspiration or orientation. Consider how many pre-teens (and twenty-somethings!) are encouraged to buy into the fashion and music "youth market." Tony Jeffs and Mark Smith argue that it is increasingly difficult to approach "youth" as a meaningful categorization. They also suggest that the concept of "youth work" that attaches to the category of "youth" may wither away.[1]

> Brian dropped into the chair exhausted. It was 11:30 P.M., and he had just got in from another Friday night club. He had been employed as a church youth worker for six months now. It had been a good night. Nearly thirty kids had turned up, around half from non-Christian homes. The games had gone well as always. Most people had joined in, though a few preferred just to flirt. The band had been great. Some of the kids had joined in enthusiastically, while others found it a bit outmoded—but then you can't cater to everyone. The talk had gone okay. He always worked hard at adapting to youth culture. His opening story had held their attention for the most part, though as usual most got fidgety when he moved into Christian application. Yes, it had all gone well. But he couldn't help wondering what had really been achieved.

Providing fun activities for young people may do some social good. Many parents like it because they fear the alternative. They would rather have their children in a church than wandering the streets. But does it nurture young people through the gospel, and does it build Christ's church? Where it is successful, most of the fruit is borne from activity around the fringes—the relationships that develop and the ad hoc conversations that ensue. Is there an alternative?

YOUNG PEOPLE AND THE WORD OF GOD

> Believing that a message wrapped in pop-culture packaging was the way to attract teens to their flocks, pastors watered down the religious content and boosted the entertainment. But in recent years churches have begun offering their young people a style of religious instruction grounded in Bible study and teachings about the doctrines of their denomination. Their conversion has been sparked by the recognition that sugar-coated Christianity, popular in the 1980s and early 1990s, has caused growing numbers of kids to turn away not just from attending youth-fellowship activities but from practicing their faith at all.[2]

That is not the conclusion of a conservative commentator but an extract from an article in *Time* magazine surveying Christian youth work in the United States.

Take a group of hormonal teenagers, put them all together in one space, and then wind them up with energetic games. It is not very realistic to expect them then to listen to a Bible talk! It is easy to suppose that attractive activities are the key to successful youth work. It is easy to suppose that the corresponding measure of success is weekly attendance. But God does his work through his word. The key to successful youth work is the Bible. This is how God does his work in young people. And the measure of success is not attendance but gospel fruit in their lives.

> Angie dropped into the chair exhausted. It was 11:30 P.M., and she had just got in from another Friday night with Hannah, Tracey, and Tracey's friend Kath. For a few weeks now she had been meeting with Hannah and Tracey every week or so. Sometimes they went shopping, sometimes they went out for coffee, and a couple of times they had been to the movies. Then they went back to Angie's apartment to study the Bible. Jo had been part of the group at the beginning but then lost interest. Hannah and Tracey were really interested—at least most of the time. And this week Tracey had brought her friend Kath along. Angie was thrilled. Being accepted at school was a big deal for Tracey; so inviting Kath had been a huge step for her. Angie spent a moment or two in prayer for the three of them before stumbling upstairs to bed.

Brian has contact with far more young people than Angie. But that does not equate to gospel contact. The numbers suggest that Brian is being more effective. But if we are convinced that the gospel changes lives, Angie's work is more significant. Her approach matches Paul's approach in 1 Thessalonians 2:8 of sharing the word and sharing your life.

YOUNG PEOPLE AND THE CHRISTIAN COMMUNITY

Compare Brian's youth-centered approach to the following true story:

Paul was a little taken aback at being asked to lead one of the small groups in the church. He did not feel equipped, and the thought of taking responsibility for such a diverse group was more than a little scary. He was reassured to learn that it would be meeting only every other week and that the church leadership recognized it was something of an "experimental" group. It was certainly unconventional. He was not a complete novice at church life, but he had never seen such a range of both ages and life settings. There were only fourteen in the group, but they included teenagers, students, unemployed people, professionals, and ex-offenders. Their meetings proved to be very interesting, but so did their social activities. The teenage boys were less than impressed when they heard about the group. But it wasn't too long before they were throwing themselves into it with a great deal of enthusiasm. They relished the opportunity to befriend and serve some of the needy members of the group. Within three months they had grown to around twenty-five people meeting regularly, and two months after that they had formed the basis of a new church plant, the first Sunday of which included three baptisms. The growth rate has now slowed down, and various pastoral difficulties have emerged, but it has proved a great setting for the discipleship of the young people. Church and mission have become default settings for them.

The intriguing aspect of this community-centered approach is that it would not be regarded as youth work, and yet it has proved successful in working with young people. Neither is it a "youth church" since the ages range from teens to middle age. It is often assumed that peer groups are key to youth ministry. Friends of ours recently left their church because there were few other teenagers in the church for their children. When they left, the other family with teenage children also left. Losing both families was a huge blow to this small church. But our experience suggests that more significant than peer relationships are relationships with Christians who are older than the teenagers but not as old as their parents—adults who may not be "youth workers" but who are committed to young people just as they are committed to other people in the church and who model gospel living and make young people feel part of the Christian community.

This takes church seriously. Integrating young people into the vibrant and diverse life of the gospel community is a key objective. It has multiple benefits. Young people belong to the extended family that is church. As such they are part of a complex network of relationships to which they contribute and from which they benefit. Of course, it is only natural for young people to default to spending time with other young people, but the church is not a "natural" agency. The church is a phenomenon that can only be explained by the operative grace of the Holy Spirit at work through the gospel of Christ. Part of the discipleship of young people is encouraging and equipping them to be willing participants in a diverse congregation.

The wider community also helps evangelize young people. Of course, young people are best placed to reach their peers with the gospel. But as we have seen, exposing people to the gospel community is a key ingredient in effective evangelism.

A further benefit of this integrated approach to reaching and discipling young people is the way they then contribute to the actual shape and color of the community. Leaders take the presence of young people actively into account as they plan the life of the church. Young people matter, not because they are the "church of tomorrow," but because they are an integral part of the church today. They too need to understand the word of God as it is taught. They need to hear the truth as it is in Christ applied to their hearts, their idols, their struggles, their joys. Listen to what Martin Luther had to say on the subject of teaching God's word to the gathered congregation:

> When I preach I don't look to the doctors and magistrates of whom there are about forty in this church. I have an eye to the many young people, children and servants of whom there are more than two thousand. I preach to these, addressing myself to their needs. If other people don't want to listen to this approach

then they can always walk out! An upright, godly and true preacher should direct his preaching to the poor, simple sort of people . . . when preachers talk to me they can show off their learning—they will be well put to their trumps! But to sprinkle Hebrew, Greek and Latin in their public sermons, suggests they are merely showing off.[3]

A willingness to apply this approach to the teaching of the gospel word is indicative of whether our evangelicalism is dynamic or merely idealistic. If the Bible is taught with the range of people in the church in mind, then it is more likely to be accessible to non-Christians whenever they are present.

But young people are not a passive audience. They play a vital part in making the church what it is called to be. Their presence should be seen as part of God's providential direction of that congregation in terms of its distinctive life and shape. Christian young people are called to be lovers of God and others just like every other Christian. The privileges and responsibilities of discipleship apply to them as much as they do to other categories of believers. Therefore their ministry is an integral part of the ministry of the local church of which they are part, and the gospel calls them to be servants in the same way as everyone else.

CHILDREN IN THE GOSPEL COMMUNITY

We are often asked what we do with children in our church plant. How can a small church have an effective children's ministry? I respond by telling the true story of a church I know. Each Sunday they had a "junior church" in the school next to the church building. Families would arrive together, and then the children up to the age of sixteen would go off to the junior church while the adults went to adult church. They only met together again at the end. This arrangement worked well for both children and adults. The children got a fun program adapted to their interests. The adults were able to meet undisturbed by fidgeting children. But at sixteen all the children left the church. I worked with one who had eventually become a Christian through another church. The children were unprepared to make the move to adult church.

Other churches encourage children to remain in the meeting throughout, expecting them to behave like little adults. Children trained in this way from an early age may pull it off, although a friend of mine admits she learned not to listen to sermons and found it difficult to break this habit as she moved into adulthood. It is completely unrealistic to expect this of unchurched families whose family life may be too chaotic to conform to this pattern. If your church manages to keep children quiet during sermons, that is probably because you are failing to bridge other social divides!

In our context we grapple with the generation gap every week. Each week we struggle to make what we do accessible to the children and relevant to adults. We adults often do not get it right: the children do not follow all that goes on, and frequently we have to put up with noisy children. But I would rather have this struggle week by week than store it up, creating an unbridgeable culture gap.

The important thing is to maintain the dual fidelity to the gospel word and the gospel community in working with children.

If the church's commitment to the word of God is both formal and dynamic, it is important for both children and adults to be sitting under the authority of the truth as it is taught. It is helpful for children to see their parents and others taking the Bible seriously and grappling with it at both the level of understanding and of obedience. One way of doing this is to have the same teaching program for the children as for the adults. Each group is then being taught at the level of their understanding, but the church as a whole is being shaped by the gospel. One church kept the children and adults together for the main teaching session and then had a specific group for children when the congregation broke into application groups. The children were led by an adult but were encouraged to take the teaching seriously and apply it to the specifics of their own hearts and issues. The person responsible for congregational teaching had to work hard at making everything accessible. But that discipline also ensured that people of any age coming in with no knowledge of the Bible were able to follow most of what was being said.

"Where is God?"
"God's everywhere."
"So is he in my tummy?"
"Er . . . yes . . . well, not really . . . well . . ."

The reason I recall this exchange with my daughter is that one of the common objections to the integration of children into the life of the community is that it sells older Christians short, depriving them of a serious engagement with truth. But two theology degrees had not adequately prepared me to tackle the metaphysical questions of a three-year-old. The questions of children, and unbelievers for that matter, force us to move beyond our erudite but superficial answers. Our jargon does not do the job. Moreover, we can no longer satisfy ourselves with a "taxing" sermon in terms of textual detail and increased knowledge as an end in itself. The gospel simply told and the Bible simply taught highlight the need in us all for godly obedience and heartfelt responsiveness to the word. The most significant and serious hermeneutical problem is not understanding but sin— our stubborn refusal to submit to the Holy Spirit as he applies his word to our hearts. The theologian Karl Barth was asked by a journalist how he would summarize the millions of words he had published. He answered without hesitation, "Jesus loves me, this I know, for the Bible tells me so."[4] Nothing could be simpler, and yet any true child of God of any age could spend an eternity meditating upon the depths of that truth along with its implications without exhausting either.

The integration of children into the life of the church is consistent with an understanding of the church as an extended family. John Driver says, "The family image constitutes one of the major biblical figures for understanding the nature and mission of the church. . . . Joachim Jeremias has called this metaphor 'Jesus' favourite image' for referring to the new people of God. . . . In Pauline thought the family image occupies the primary role in his reflection on the nature and mission of the messianic community."[5]

We have a simple rule of thumb in our church: if we would do this as family, we can do it as church; if we would not do this as family, why do it as church? This is not intended to cover every possible eventuality, but it has proved useful in maintaining a church life that is refreshingly simple and uncluttered, with space for relationships and front-line evangelism. But these pragmatic benefits are only favorable consequences; the principle of church as family is primary. Mutual responsibility between the generations is normative for family life and the way in which values are transmitted. Should that not be normative for church also? As those relationships develop and grow over the years, and as the child moves into adolescence, the strength of those intergenerational friendships can be powerful means of grace. In the purposes of God they can be ways of keeping the young adult from becoming one among the hundreds who leave our churches each week never to return.

SUCCESS

HIS FRUSTRATION WAS OBVIOUS as we drove together. I was sharing the car with a pastor whose church of eighty or so had recently planted a new congregation. Another area of their town was without an evangelical church. Convinced that church planting was the best way to reach this area, they had planted a church at some considerable cost to themselves. But their plans had been vociferously opposed by a well-known figure in the evangelical world. His church of several hundred in the next town included people driving the fifteen-minute journey from the targeted area. And he did not want his church being weakened. "He thinks he is being successful," my friend said with an exasperated tone, "because he has a church of five hundred that is growing. But they're not reaching anyone with the gospel. They're just sucking in Christians from all around."

If we are to reach our cities and towns effectively with the gospel through church planting, then we need a radically different model of success. Too many of our notions of success owe more to the world than to the God we worship. We measure success in terms of numbers, budgets, style, staff, prestige. We are not quite as crass as to think the church leader with the biggest salary and the flashiest car is the most successful. But we are not far from thinking that the church leader with the biggest congregation and the flashiest Sunday meetings is the most successful. The following real conversation took place during a conference organizational meeting in which Steve was involved:

Steve: We could invite X to speak.

Committee member: I don't think so. He doesn't have a big enough congregation.

Steve: What do you mean?

Committee member: People only want to hear successful speakers with large congregations.

Steve: Let me be clear on what you're saying. As things stand you wouldn't have me speak because I lead a small church plant. But if tomorrow I moved to lead a church with several hundred members, then you would have me speak?

Committee member: Yes.

Steve: Even though I personally wouldn't have changed in any way or achieved anything new?

Committee member: Yes.

In this chapter we will consider:

- two competing models of *growth*: larger congregations versus more congregations
- two competing models of *leadership*: leadership as performance versus leadership as enabling
- two competing models of *success*: a church of glory versus a church of the cross

TWO MODELS OF GROWTH: LARGER VERSUS MORE

People value large congregations because size is how we measure success. But we must not confuse large with successful. Nor for that matter should we equate small with successful! As we have already argued, smaller groups make it easier for the "one anothering" commended in the New Testament to take place. But despite our preference for small churches, we do not want to suggest that large churches are wrong, nor diminish all the good gospel work that they do. We recognize that there are some things larger churches can do more effectively than smaller ones. Let us celebrate the different models that exist within evangelicalism.

But we do want to question the assumption that big is necessarily better. It may not be so. Bigger congregations are sometimes, though by no means always, the result of two possible failures:

A Gospel Failure

It is actually not that difficult to create a large congregation. Paul tells us how. You give people what will "suit their own desires" and say "what their itching ears want to hear" (2 Timothy 4:3). Entertain the congregation each Sunday with a good performance. Do not focus on the depth of their sin, nor the cost of cross-centered discipleship. Whatever you do, do not challenge the idolatrous desires of their hearts. Instead offer them sermons on how to realize those desires and find success in life. Or better still, tell amusing stories that excite them with a vague sense of optimism. That is one way to grow a congregation.

But Paul also tells Timothy to keep his head. There is a more godly way that is faithful to the gospel. Timothy is to "preach the Word . . . in season and out of season." He is to stick with "sound doctrine." He is to correct and rebuke as well as encourage, even if it means enduring hardship (vv. 2–5). Paul gives Timothy this charge in view of the coming of Christ Jesus "who will judge the living and the dead" (v. 1). Christ's judgment is not a truth that itching ears want to hear, but it is the constant backdrop to true Christian ministry. We must be gospel-centered, even though the world around us wants to be centered on everything but the gospel. This may well make us less successful, but only if we measure success in terms of numbers. If you view success in a biblical way—as faithfulness to Christ and his word—then being gospel-centered becomes the very definition of success.

Obviously most large evangelical churches remain faithful to the gospel. Large does not equal unfaithful. But Paul's teaching in 2 Timothy 4 does remind us that numbers are not a reliable or sufficient measure of success.

A Community Failure

Fresh out of university, my wife and I moved to a suburb of London and started looking for a church to join. Our one contact in the area attended a large, well-known evangelical church. He had been attending the church for over two years. And yet, he told us, if he sat on the other side of the church building from his normal spot, people would ask him if he was a newcomer.

The Bible calls the church a family. It describes the church as a community that shares together. The church is a body whose members perfectly fit together. We belong to one another. Our friend's church was neither a family nor a community. It had no vision for involvement in its immediate community. The truth is, it was not really a church according to any New Testament definition. It was a preaching center. You drove to their large parking garage for your weekly dose of religion just as you traveled to the out-of-town supermarket for your weekly groceries.

Living plants are growing plants. The plants in my garden are either growing or dying. In the same way living churches are growing churches. Members will grow in their love for God and for one another. Unbelievers will encounter the aroma of Christ. Such growth is rarely straightforward. Often it is three steps forward and two steps backward. But growth is normal. God's word will achieve what he purposes for it. And so, as people are saved, the church will grow numerically.

But numerical growth need not equate to larger congregations. There is another model for church growth: growing churches by planting churches. As we have argued, planting churches offers the most biblical and most effective way to reach our towns and cities for Christ. But it requires a different vision for church growth. If we measure ourselves by the size of our congregations, there will always be a strong deterrent to plant.

TWO MODELS OF LEADERSHIP: PERFORMANCE VERSUS ENABLING

More and more I hear stories of ministers who are struggling to cope with the pressure of having to do well week after week. I hear stories of ministers who are struggling with sin and temptation but have no one in their congregation to whom to turn, forcing them constantly to pretend. Part of the problem is a view of ministry as performance. Services, sermons, vision, administration, publications must all be maintained to a high standard. And the measure of that standard is not simply whether the word is shaping the life of the church and the lives of its members. The measure is the quality of the performance—a certain style of service and sermon, with the exact nature of that style varying within different evangelical traditions. Even the architecture of our buildings reinforces the message: there is an audience, and there is a performer.

There is another model of leadership—the model of leadership as enabling. In Ephesians 4:11–13 Paul says, "It was [Christ] who gave some to be apostles, some to be prophets, some to be evangelists, and some to be pastors and teachers, to prepare God's people for works of service, so that the body of Christ may be built up until we all reach unity in the faith and in the knowledge of the Son of God and become mature, attaining to the whole measure of the fullness of Christ." Paul highlights the role of those who proclaim and apply God's word because, as we have seen, the word is central to Christian growth and experience. But notice that these leaders do not do the work of God in the church. Their role is to equip God's people for works of service. It is all God's people who do the works of service so that the body of Christ may be built up.[1] New Testament leaders do not fulfill the roles of priest or king because those roles are fulfilled in Christ. Jesus is our Priest and King, while all believers together form a priestly kingdom (1 Peter 2:9; Revelation 1:6). We work together to become Christ's body. We work with, and for, one another so that together we can be mature and Christlike.

Leadership as performance reflects a professionalization of leadership. The minister is usually an outsider brought into the congregation. If he is not up to standard, he can be replaced; so star performers are much sought after. The key issue seems to be the impression pastors create in an interview or a pulpit—their pizzazz. But character, not charisma, is central to biblical criteria. A university education, oratory, personal magnetism, and perceived dynamism are not listed by Paul as significant factors (1 Timothy 3 and Titus 1). Leaders are those who believe, teach, and live the gospel in the daily routine of their lives. That can only be discerned through prolonged exposure to their lives. They are recognized rather than appointed. They are people already taking initiative in the life of the church—building relationships with non-Christians, encouraging others, setting an example of godliness, praying in the prayer meeting. The primary mistake I have made in bringing people into leadership has been a failure to recognize that character is revealed in the details of a person's life. It is too easy to be blinded by gifts. Simply because someone is an able Bible teacher, for example, does not mean he will be a good leader. We need to look for integrity. Does he keep his promises? Is he committed to people? Does he care for his family?

In the New Testament, church leaders were appointed from within the congregation. They were church members before they were church leaders. And this did not change when they became leaders. They were sheep more than shepherds. "Who pastors the pastors?" people often ask and sometimes set up hierarchical structures in response. But the question assumes a false distinction between the minister and the congregation.

I am pastored by my congregation. My struggles are often out in the open for everyone to see. I can be honest about my failures. Like other members of the congregation, not every sin of mine is common knowledge, but there are certain people who know the idols of my heart, who challenge me regularly and ask the difficult questions. In this context I have been able to deal with sins that had gone unaddressed for many years. In the process I model, not a false perfection, but "progress" (1 Timothy 4:15). I model the grace of God rather than the goodness of me. My leadership is in no way undermined as a result. Rather it is enhanced. People approach me with their struggles because they know me to be a fellow struggler and a fellow recipient of grace.

I don't feel the pressure to "perform" for two reasons. First, "success" and "failure" are common property. We all share a sense of responsibility for what happens. We use first-person pronouns rather than second-person pronouns: "we could have done better" rather than "you could have done better." If I am negligent or ungodly, then people will challenge me. But I do not have to perform. Second, ministry is not an event that occurs on a Sunday. It is a lifestyle of word-centered activity. Success is not judged by a sermon or service. It is judged in terms of growing Christians and gospel opportunities.

I have used the first person, but not to trumpet my experience. The reality is that it is often very messy. I have used the first person to show that what I am describing is not impossible rhetoric or unrealistic idealism. I remember talking over lunch with two church leaders. At first they expressed concern that we did not have an accountability structure over and outside us. But as I talked to them about the day-to-day accountability I enjoy from my congregation and from other congregational leaders with its opportunities to share heart struggles, their attitude changed. Soon they were saying, "I wish we had something like this. Our accountability is so superficial. I feel alone most of the time." True accountability is more about relationships than about hierarchies. It requires community more than structures. The sad thing was that those two church leaders could not imagine their situation ever changing.

Church without programs, structures, or buildings can make you very vulnerable. Leadership in which your life is open can feel scary. But we should embrace this fragility because it forces us to trust God's sovereign grace.

I often describe our church as a group of messy people led by messy people. That is what happens when you take away performance and pretense. They are replaced by messy pastoral issues. But this is how growth takes place. This is how grace is displayed. To paraphrase the opening words of the Sermon on the Mount, "Blessed are the broken people, for the kingdom of heaven belongs to them" (Matthew 5:3). Ministry as performance does not welcome brokenness because it ruins the veneer. But God's kingdom is for broken people. When pastoral problems emerge, I do not think, "Oh no, here's another problem to solve." I think, "What a privilege to be serving broken people. This is where God's blessing is found."

The real tragedy of leadership as performance is that it devalues the work of Christ. Our identity then is not rooted in grace but in the success of our ministry. And so we feel upbeat when we have performed well, and we feel down when things are not going well. We become enslaved to other people's approval. We are concerned to prove ourselves, and that is just another way of talking about self-justification. We preach justification by faith on the day of judgment but do not practice justification by faith in the daily routine of our lives. Our practical theology has become disconnected from our confessional theology. Our song becomes:

> *My hope is built on something less*
> *Than Jesus' blood and righteousness;*
> *I trust my skills, I trust my fame,*
> *And maybe sometimes Jesus' name.*

But we cannot keep it up. Self-justification is always beyond us. The chorus of Edward Mote's hymn, which I have taken the liberty of inverting, actually goes: "On Christ, the solid Rock, I stand; all other ground is sinking sand." Leadership as performance is sinking sand.

TWO MODELS OF SUCCESS: GLORY VERSUS THE CROSS

It is tempting for us to think that what we need most are national evangelistic campaigns or megachurches with slick presentations or media attention and political influence. But Jesus says the kingdom of God has been given to his "little flock" (Luke 12:32). At the heart of Jesus' future are not national or global structures but small, unassuming churches—Christ's little flock. And to Christ's little flock the all-powerful, life-giving rule of God has been given.

As we have seen, Martin Luther distinguished between a theology of glory and a theology of the cross. The theology of glory seeks the revelation of God in the power and glory of his actions. The theology of the cross sees the ultimate revelation of God in the cross. By faith we see in the cross power in weakness, wisdom in folly, and glory in shame. This was the foundational principle of the Reformation's theological method.

We need to develop a corresponding understanding of "the church of the cross," of which the phrase "Christ's little flock" is an image. We have borrowed the term "church of the cross" from Emil Brunner, who says:

> The whole history of Christianity, and the history of the world as a whole, would have followed a different course if it had not been that again and again a theology of the cross became the theology of glory, and that the church of the cross became a church of glory.[2]

The church is always tempted toward a church of glory, whether that takes the form of grand buildings, political influence, global structures, charismatic personalities, or megachurches. But an approach to the church consistent with the gospel of Christ crucified and discipleship shaped by that gospel is an ecclesiology of the cross. That means power in weakness, wisdom in folly, and glory in shame. It means we must put our confidence in Christ's little flock and the sovereign rule of God. It means we must put our energies into the church of the cross even if that means obscurity.

The problem is that "power . . . made perfect in weakness" (2 Corinthians 12:9) is so counterintuitive and countercultural that we do not believe it. We believe that God will use the powerful and important and impressive. But he does not. We need a radical change of perspective. We need to ditch our worldly notions of success. We need to ditch our modernistic preoccupation with numbers and size. We need to turn our notions of success upside down so that we align them with God's kingdom perspective.

[Jesus] also said, "This is what the kingdom of God is like. A man scatters seed on the ground. Night and day, whether he sleeps or gets up, the seed sprouts and grows, though he does not know how. All by itself the soil produces corn—first the stalk, then the head, then the full grain in the head. As soon as the grain is ripe, he puts the sickle to it, because the harvest has come."

Again he said, "What shall we say the kingdom of God is like, or what parable shall we use to describe it? It is like a mustard seed, which is the smallest seed you plant in the ground. Yet when planted, it grows and becomes the largest of all garden plants, with such big branches that the birds of the air can perch in its shade." (Mark 4:26–32)

On the final day, what is unseen will be revealed (Mark 4:21–23), and what is small will fill the earth. But in the present, God's kingdom is secret. It grows unseen. It is small in the eyes of this world. We need to trust God's word and God's reign. Success is not defined in terms of what can be seen, for God's kingdom is unseen. The crown of righteousness is given not to those who have led large congregations, but to those like Paul who can say, "I have fought the good fight, I have finished the race, I have kept the faith" (2 Timothy 4:7–8). Success is to be faithful to Christ and his word.

A Christian friend of mine was talking with a social worker in a poor area of London. This social worker is a Marxist, so he has no particular sympathy for Christianity. My friend asked him whether the church made much of an impact in the community in which he worked. The social worker said, "If you mean the public face of the church—its pronouncement, its projects, and its initiatives—then the answer is resoundingly no. But if you took away all the kindnesses and neighborly acts that Christians do—visiting the sick, shopping for the housebound, and so on—then this community would fall apart." The world does not normally see this. But it is God's kingdom at work. René Padilla, the Latin American missiologist, said:

One of the greatest challenges we Christians have at the threshold of the third millennium is the articulation and practical implementation of an ecclesiology that views the local church, and particularly the church of the poor, as the primary agent of holistic mission. Such a thesis may not be readily accepted by people who have made of "development" among the poor a life career. It is essential, however, to the task of facilitating, in response to God's call, the practice of holistic mission among the greatest possible number of local churches—and let us remember that the large majority of local churches around the world are poor, indeed, very poor—that they may be "the salt of the earth" and "the light of the world."[3]

The future of mission does not lie in grand strategies or meta-structures. Christ is building his church, for the most part unseen, in the shape of thousands of small congregations. This is the future of the church—the sovereignty of the risen Christ and "the church of the poor."

Working with students and professionals, it is easy to suppose that pastoral problems can be addressed through well-honed arguments or that mission can be conducted through well-practiced techniques. But this is a delusion. It is a delusion that has been shattered for me as I have worked with more marginal people whose lives are less ordered and whose reactions are less predictable. But then as the leader of another congregation said to me, "It's been shattered for me by working with high-achieving, middle-class twenty-somethings!" Whatever our context, we serve faithfully and diligently, but God alone "builds the house" (Psalm 127:1). We are wholly dependent on the sovereign grace of God. There is only one key to successful ministry, and it is in God's hands. In the light of sovereign grace, we work, we pray, and we do not lose heart.

Pachuca is about an hour's drive north of Mexico City—a city of around one million people originally built by the British to service local mines. The British have been long gone, leaving behind three things. First, soccer—it was through Pachuca that soccer first came to Mexico. Second, Cornish pasties—there is a small part of Mexico that serves Cornish pasties, albeit spicy Cornish pasties with chili. And third, a town clock with the same internal mechanism as Big

Ben. When I pointed out that it was not working, my hosts shrugged their shoulders and said, "Mexican time!"

I had come to Pachuca to see the Arms of Mercy church and its work with local children. Located on the outskirts of the city at the top of a windswept hill, the church meets in a tin shack with broken chairs and homemade wooden benches. A few yards away there is a dilapidated hut where they provide an after-school club and meals to around seventy local children. Many of the local homes have no water or electricity, and because of its location the area gets very cold in winter. It is a cliché, I know, but the strength of their welcome was truly humbling. I felt as if I had reached the edge of the world. We stood on the barren outskirts of the city, but also in a symbolic sense at the margins of the world. And here at the edge was a little piece of God's kingdom. Here at the edge Christ's "arms of mercy" were held open through the work of his church. And this reality, largely unseen by the world, is replicated a million times across the globe. Small, poor, unseen, but this is success. These people are the heroes of heaven. This is the future of the church.

CONCLUSION:
A PASSION FOR GOD

THIS BOOK HAS SUGGESTED changes that could, and should, be made to the life and mission of the church. But the future of the church does not lie in changing its structures. Far more important than any ecclesiastical or missiological innovations is a passion for God. All the principles and suggestions we have put forward are empty without this. The glory of God and the grace of God are the heartbeat of Christian life and mission.

We have presented a vision that places the gospel word and the gospel community at the center of Christian practice. We have spoken of this as a dual fidelity because it describes what it means to be biblically faithful. We have attempted to show what this dual fidelity might involve in different areas of the Christian life and mission.

But our proposals should not be viewed as a recipe for success nor a guarantee of authentic ministry. Christianity is not a strategy or a set of principles. It is a relationship of love with the Triune God. The gospel word and the gospel community must be central to Christian practice. But our hearts should be fixed on the grace of God, the love of God, and the glory of God. The only true center of Christian existence is God himself.

Many people are excited by new forms of church or new forms of mission. In some circles *community* is a bit of a buzzword. But we will only create authentic Christian community or mission if we begin—and keep on beginning—with the grace of God. Community may sound exciting in theory, but in practice it is also painful and messy. When you share your lives with people, you can be sure you will annoy one another! But grace makes us humble. It prevents us from boasting or thinking ourselves superior. Grace makes us loving. It reminds us of God's love to us, and it reminds us of God's love to our brothers and sisters. How can I avoid or despise or patronize those for whom Christ shed his blood (Acts 20:28)? Grace is the foundation of community-building.

It was Augustine who first summarized the Christian life with the words, "Love God and do as you please." The older we get, the more we are persuaded by that deceptively simple maxim. Paul says:

> *If I speak in the tongues of men and of angels, but have not love, I am only a resounding gong or a clanging cymbal. If I have the gift of prophecy and can fathom all mysteries and all knowledge, and if I have a faith that can move mountains, but have not love, I am nothing. If I give all I possess to the poor and surrender my body to the flames, but have not love, I gain nothing. (1 Corinthians 13:1–3)*

If we are culturally relevant, we might add, but have not love, we gain nothing. If we preach the finest sermons but have not love, we are resounding gongs. Indeed, if we write books about mission and church but have not love, we are just clanging cymbals! Attendance at meetings, involvement in evangelism, an ability to handle the Bible, starting new initiatives, a reputation for being sound (or radical)—all of these, in and of themselves, indicate nothing unless they are a heart response to the deep, passionate love *of* God and emerge out of a deep, passionate love *for* God.

Thomas Chalmers, the nineteenth-century Scottish minister, preached an extraordinary sermon entitled "The Expulsive Power of a New Affection." In it he argued that in order for us as Christians not to love the world, we must love God more. Love for the world is the affection to which our hearts default and from which we will be weaned only by a greater affection.

> [The gospel] brings for admittance to the very door of our heart, an affection which once seated upon its throne, will either subordinate every previous inmate, or bid it away. . . . In the gospel we

so behold God, as that we may love God. It is then, and then only, when God stands revealed as an object of confidence to sinners and when our desire after him is not chilled into apathy. . . . It is when he stands dismantled of the terrors which belong to him as an offended lawgiver and when we are enabled by faith, which is his own gift, to see his glory in the face of Jesus Christ, and to hear his beseeching voice, as it protests good will to men, and entreats the return of all who will to a full pardon and a gracious acceptance . . . *it is then, that a love paramount to the love of the world, and at length expulsive of it, first arises in the regenerated bosom.* It is when released from the spirit of bondage with which love cannot dwell, and when admitted into the number of God's children through the faith that is in Christ Jesus, the spirit of adoption is poured upon us—*it is then that the heart, brought under the mastery of one great and predominant affection, is delivered from the tyranny of its former desires, in the only way in which deliverance is possible.*[1]

Chalmers's insight is compelling in its simplicity. Love for God is the great effect of the gospel. The love produced by the good news concerning Christ is so effective that our heart is captured and secured. It is this love that makes the world less attractive and enables us to resist the temptations of sin. And so time and again we go back to the gospel of God the Father, Son, and Holy Spirit. We must refocus our minds and hearts on him in all his redeeming glory. When others are struggling with sin, do not allow the sin to preoccupy you. Remind them of the God they worship, and bring them to the cross where he is seen in all of his glorious love, holiness, and grace.

Chalmers was not afraid to speak of the gospel as the place where we "behold God." In contrast we sometimes speak of the gospel as though it were nothing more than a series of propositions to which we give intellectual assent. But the gospel is not mere information about Christ: he himself *is* the good news! It is in and through this gospel word that God gives "the light of the knowledge of the glory of God in the face of Christ" (2 Corinthians 4:6).

There is a lot of talk today of "gospel ministers," "gospel

work," "gospel churches," and so on. There are some good reasons for this use of the word *gospel* since other definitions of identity are proving inadequate. But we need to be careful not to depersonalize our faith. In believing in the gospel we believe in Jesus Christ. To be gospel-centered is to be Jesus-centered. A gospel worker is a servant of Jesus Christ. We must not reduce Christianity to intellectual arguments or principles of ministry, however gospel-hyphenated they are. Our focus must be on the Father, the Son, and the Spirit.

I love being married, but I love being married because it unites me with my wife. In the same way, I love the gospel, but I love the gospel because it unites me with my Savior. We are not saved by principles or strategies but by a person. Propositional truth is important, the suspicions of postmodernism notwithstanding. But propositional truth is important because it points me to the person who is the Truth and with whom I have a relationship by grace. When my heart was opened to the gospel as it was preached to me as a child, I came face-to-face with Christ himself. True gospel preaching warms my heart because as I hear it, the Holy Spirit is bringing Christ to me once more, and once more he wins my heart.

Have you noticed how possible it is to speak about doctrine and yet remain reluctant to speak of the Savior in intimate terms? I find it easy to speak with other Christians about mission or church. I can talk all day about the exegetical complexities of Romans 7. I enjoy nothing more than a lengthy discussion of some point of doctrine. But I find myself stumbling when conversation drifts toward Jesus! I suspect I am not alone. I have been attending conferences for more than twenty-five years; yet rarely have conversations in those meetings turned towards the loveliness of the Savior. What a tragic irony! One of the great glories of the new covenant is that it consists of personal possessive pronouns: Jesus is *my* Savior and *my* Lord; to *me* he is the all-together lovely one and the fairest of ten thousand! Consider Paul's great boast: "I live by faith in the Son of God, who loved *me* and gave himself for *me*" (Galatians 2:20).

Peter encapsulates this glory and intimacy in the opening chapter of his first letter. The apostle writes about the "living hope" into which we have been born again (v. 3). That hope concerns an imperishable, undefiled, and unfading inheritance (vv. 4–5). This life will involve suffering in which our faith is tested and tried, so that it will result in God's praise when Jesus is finally revealed in glory (vv. 6–7). In the meantime, as we wait we love him, believe in him, and "are filled with an inexpressible and glorious joy" (v. 8).

This is why the gospel word and the gospel community are essential. My heart needs to hear that word often if it is to be filled with "inexpressible and glorious joy." It is among the community of God's people that the word will be brought to bear on my life frequently and perceptively. It is through his word and among his people that the Holy Spirit works to break this sinner's heart and renew it so that I love God truly, madly, and deeply.

NOTES

Introduction

1. John Stott, *The Living Church* (Nottingham, UK: Inter-Varsity Press, 2007), p. 58.

Chapter 1: Why Gospel?

1. Christopher J. H. Wright, *The Mission of God: Unlocking the Bible's Grand Narrative* (Nottingham, UK: Inter-Varsity Press, 2006). Cited in Christopher J. H. Wright, "The Mission of God," *Evangelicals Now* (December 2006).
2. Mark Greene and Tracy Cotterell, *Let My People Grow* (London: LICC, 2005), p. 3.
3. Ibid., pp. 3–4.
4. Ibid., p. 5.

Chapter 2: Why Community?

1. Sinclair B. Ferguson, *Grow in Grace* (Edinburgh: Banner of Truth, 1989), p. 67.
2. John Stott, *The Living Church* (Nottingham, UK: Inter-Varsity Press, 2007), pp. 19–20.
3. See Tim Chester, *Delighting in the Trinity* (Oxford, UK: Monarch, 2005), pp. 159–173.
4. The Crowded House Core Values (http://www.thecrowdedhouse.org/?q=ourvalues).
5. Robert Martin-Achard, cited in Johannes Blauw, *The Missionary Nature of the Church* (Cambridge, UK: Lutterworth, 1962), p. 33.

Chapter 3: Evangelism

1. John Calvin, *Calvin's Commentaries: The Second Epistle of Paul the Apostle to the Corinthians and the Epistles to Timothy, Titus and Philemon*, trans. T. A. Smail (Edinburgh: St. Andrew Press, 1964), p. 231.
2. Cited in Timothy George, *Theology of the Reformers* (Leicester, UK: Apollos, 1988), p. 89.
3. Don Carson, *The Gospel According to John* (Nottingham, UK: Inter-Varsity Press, 1991), p. 481.
4. Lesslie Newbigin, *The Gospel in a Pluralist Society* (London: SPCK, 1989), pp. 222–233.
5. John Stott, *The Message of Ephesians* (Nottingham, UK: Inter-Varsity Press, 1979), p. 123.

Chapter 4: Social Involvement

1. Cited in David Cannadine, *Class in Britain* (New Haven, CT: Yale, 1998), pp. 20, ix.

2. See Tim Chester, *Good News to the Poor* (Nottingham, UK: Inter-Varsity Press, 2004), Chapter 4.

3. Cited in Paul Vallely, "Mrs Jones has Something to Say," *The Independent* (August 7, 1996).

4. Robert Chambers, *Rural Development: Putting the Last First* (Warwickshire, UK: Intermediate Technology, 1983).

5. See, for example, David Archer and Sara Cottingham, *Action Research Report on REFLECT* (DFID Education Research No. 17, 1996); Robert Chambers, *Whose Reality Counts? Putting the First Last* (Warwickshire, UK: Intermediate Technology, 1997); Anne Hope and Sally Timmel, *Training for Transformation: A Handbook for Community Workers, Books I, II and III* (Warwickshire, UK: Intermediate Technology, 1984); David C. Korten, *Getting to the 21st Century: Voluntary Action and the Global Agenda* (Bloomfield, CT: Kumarian Press, 1990); Bryant Myers, *Walking with the Poor* (Maryknoll, NY: Orbis, 1999); Jules N. Pretty, Irene Guijt, John Thompson, and Ian Scoones, *Participatory Learning and Action: A Trainer's Guide* (Edinburgh: IIED, 1995).

6. See Tim Chester, *Delighting in the Trinity* (Oxford, UK: Monarch, 2005), Chapter 10.

Chapter 5: Church Planting

1. On Paul's use of the terms *church* and *churches*, see Robert Banks, *Paul's Idea of Community* (Carlisle, UK: Paternoster, 1980), pp. 33–52, and Peter O'Brien, "A Note on the Term *Ecclesia* in Colossians and Philemon," *Colossians, Philemon*, WBC (Nashville: Word, 1982), pp. 57–61.

2. Lesslie Newbigin, *The Gospel in a Pluralist Society* (London: SPCK, 1989), p. 227.

3. Ibid., pp. 232–233.

4. Stuart Murray, *Church Planting: Laying Foundations* (Carlisle, UK: Paternoster, 1998), p. 32.

5. C. Peter Wagner, *Church Planting for a Greater Harvest* (Ventura, CA: Regal Books, 1990).

6. Martin Robinson and David Spriggs, *Church Planting: The Training Manual* (Oxford, UK: Lynx, 1995).

7. Derek Tidball, *An Introduction to the Sociology of the New Testament* (Carlisle, UK: Paternoster, 1983), pp. 79–86, and Robert Banks, *Paul's Idea of Community* (Carlisle, UK: Paternoster, 1980), pp. 33–42.

8. Carolyn Osiek and David L. Balch, *Families in the New Testament World: Household and House Churches* (Louisville: Westminster John Knox Press, 1997), pp. 5–35.

9. Bradley Blue, "Acts and the House Church," *The Book of Acts in Its First-Century Setting, Volume 2: The Graeco-Roman Setting*, eds. David W. J. Gill and Conrad Gempf (Carlisle, UK: Paternoster, 1999), pp. 119–222.

10. We see the same pattern in Romans 1:7; 16:3, 5, 10–11; Philippians 4:22; Colossians 4:15–16; and Philemon 1–2.

11. See Scott Bartchy, "Table Fellowship," *Dictionary of Jesus and the Gospels* (Nottingham, UK: Inter-Varsity Press, 1992), pp. 796–800.

12. Figures from Philip Richter and Leslie Francis, *Gone But Not Forgotten* (London: DLT, 1998).

Chapter 6: World Mission

1. Vinoth Ramachandra, *The Recovery of Mission: Beyond the Pluralist Paradigm* (Carlisle, UK: Paternoster, 2002), p. 224.
2. See Tim Chester and Steve Timmis, *The World We All Want* (Carlisle, UK: Authentic Media, 2005).
3. C. F. Keil and F. Delitzsch, *Commentary on the Old Testament, Volume 3: The Pentateuch* (Edinburgh: T. & T. Clark, 1870), p. 2.
4. Leon Morris, *The Epistle to the Romans* (Grand Rapids, MI: Eerdmans, 1988), p. 514.
5. David J. Bosch, *Transforming Mission: Paradigm Shifts in Theology of Mission* (Maryknoll, NY: Orbis, 1991), p. 332.
6. Markus Bockmuehl, *The Epistle to the Philippians* (Peabody, MA: Hendrickson, 1998), pp. 96–97.

Chapter 7: Discipleship and Training

1. G. K. Chesterton, *Heretics* (public domain), p. 59.
2. Henri Nouwen, cited in Philip Yancey, "Keep it in the Family," *The Briefing*, No. 195 (February 1997), p. 10.
3. Yancey, ibid.
4. Quotes from Jules N. Pretty, Irene Guijt, John Thompson, and Ian Scoones, *Participatory Learning and Action* (Edinburgh: IIED, 1995), p. 1.
5. Peter Adam, *Hearing God's Words* (Leicester, UK: Apollos, 2004), p. 53.
6. Christopher J. H. Wright, *Deuteronomy* (Peabody, MA: Hendrickson, 1996), p. 99.
7. Ibid., p. 100.
8. Jay Adams, *A Theology of Christian Counseling* (Grand Rapids, MI: Zondervan, 1979), pp. 89–91.

Chapter 8: Pastoral Care

1. Parts of this material first appeared in the Open Bible Institute Pastoral Care module and are adapted with permission.
2. Frank Furedi, *Therapy Culture: Cultivating Vulnerability in an Uncertain Age* (New York: Routledge, 2003).
3. Paul Gascoigne, *Being Gazza: My Journey to Hell and Back* (London: Headline, 2006).
4. Paul Gascoigne, "Sobering Tale of How Gazza Fell Back into the Grip of Addiction," *The Times*, May 20, 2006.
5. John Calvin, *Calvin's Commentaries: Hebrews and 1 & 2 Peter*, trans. William B. Johnston (Edinburgh: St. Andrew Press, 1963), p. 330.
6. R. C. Lucas and C. Green, *The Message of 2 Peter and Jude* (Nottingham, UK: Inter-Varsity Press, 1995), p. 48.

7. Richard Winter, *The Roots of Sorrow* (Basingstoke, UK: Marshall, Morgan & Scott, 1985), p. 36.

8. Jonathan Edwards, *Charity and Its Fruits* (Edinburgh: Banner of Truth, 1978), p. 79.

Chapter 9: Spirituality

1. John Calvin, *Institutes of the Christian Religion*, trans. F. L. Battles, ed. J. T. McNeill (London: Westminster/SCM, 1961), 3.20.11.

2. William Lane, *Hebrews 1–8* (Nashville: Word, 1991), p. 87.

Chapter 10: Theology

1. Herman Bavinck, *The Doctrine of God* (Edinburgh: Banner of Truth, 1977), back cover.

2. John Calvin, *Calvin's Commentaries,* Volume XXI (Grand Rapids, MI: Baker, 1979), pp. 249–250.

3. Ibid., p. 249.

4. David J. Bosch, *Transforming Mission: Paradigm Shifts in Theology of Mission* (Maryknoll, NY: Orbis, 1991), p. 494.

5. René Padilla, *Mission Between the Times* (Grand Rapids, MI: Eerdmans, 1985), p. 89.

6. David Smith, *Crying in the Wilderness: Evangelism and Mission in Today's Culture* (Carlisle, UK: Paternoster, 2000), pp. 21–22.

7. John Howard Yoder, "The Hermeneutics of Anabaptism," *Mennonite Quarterly Review* (October 1967), p. 301.

8. Don Cupitt, *Taking Leave of God* (London: SCM, 1980), p. ix.

9. Ibid., p. 4.

10. John Calvin, *Institutes of the Christian Religion*, trans. F. L. Battles, ed. J. T. McNeill (London: Westminster/SCM, 1961), 3.6.4.

Chapter 11: Apologetics

1. Cited in Friedrich Paulsen, *Introduction to Philosophy* (New York: Holt, 1922), p. 10.

2. Stephen Williams, *Revelation and Reconciliation: A Window on Modernity* (Cambridge, UK: Cambridge University Press, 1995), p. 8.

3. Friedrich Nietzsche, *Beyond Good and Evil*, cited in Williams, *Revelation and Reconciliation*, p. 9.

4. Aldous Huxley, *Ends and Means* (London: Chatto & Windus, 1937), pp. 272–273.

5. For further examples, see Tony Payne and Phillip D. Jenson, *Pure Sex* (Sydney: Matthias Media, 1998), Chapter 4.

6. Friedrich Nietzsche, *The Gay Science*, trans. W. Kaufmann (New York: Vintage Books, 1974), III.125.

7. Guy Deutscher, *The Unfolding of Language* (London: Heinemann, 2005); cited in Deborah Cameron, "Forked Tongues," *The Guardian Review* (July 2, 2005), p. 14.

8. Graham Tomlin, *The Power of the Cross: Theology and the Death of Christ in Paul, Luther and Pascal* (Carlisle, UK: Paternoster, 1999), pp. 241–242.

9. Ibid., pp. 249–250.

10. Richard Sibbes, "The Bruised Reed and Smoking Flax," in *Works of Richard Sibbes*, Vol. 1 (Edinburgh: Banner of Truth, 1973), p. 89.

11. Ibid., p. 82.

12. Cited in Williams, *Revelation and Reconciliation*, p. 6.

13. Cited in Randy Frazee, *The Connecting Church* (Grand Rapids, MI: Zondervan, 2001), p. 85.

14. Christopher J. H. Wright, *Living as the People of God* (Nottingham, UK: Inter-Varsity Press, 1983), pp. 40–41.

15. Yann Martel, *Life of Pi* (Edinburgh: Canongate, 2002), p. 317.

16. Graham Tomlin, *The Provocative Church* (London: SPCK, 2004), p. 12.

Chapter 12: Children and Young People

1. Tony Jeffs and Mark Smith, "The Problem of 'Youth' for Youth Work," *Youth and Policy*, 62 (1999), pp. 45–66.

2. Sonja Steptoe, "In Touch With Jesus," *Time* magazine, (October 31, 2006).

3. Adapted from Martin Luther, *Table Talk* (London: H. G. Bohn, 1857), CCCCXX-VII.

4. Mark Galli, *131 Christians Everyone Should Know* (Nashville: Broadman & Holman, 2000), p. 48.

5. John Driver, *Images of Church in Mission* (Scottdale, PA: Herald Press, 1997), p. 139.

Chapter 13: Success

1. For a more detailed discussion of the exegetical controversies in these verses, see Peter T. O'Brien, *The Letter to the Ephesians* (Grand Rapids, MI: Eerdmans/Leicester, UK: Apollos, 1999), pp. 297–305, and Harold W. Hoehner, *Ephesians: An Exegetical Commentary* (Grand Rapids, MI: Baker, 2002), pp. 547–551.

2. Emil Brunner, *The Mediator* (Cambridge, UK: Lutterworth, 1934), p. 435.

3. C. René Padilla, "The Church of the Poor" (unpublished paper, 1999).

Conclusion

1. Adapted from Thomas Chalmers, "The Expulsive Power of a New Affection" (London: Hatchard, 1861), emphasis added.

SCRIPTURE INDEX

GENERAL INDEX